vampires
v
werewolves

THE VAMPIRES

vampires

v

werewolves

THE VAMPIRES

MARTIN HOWDEN

JOHN BLAKE

Published by John Blake Publishing Ltd,
3 Bramber Court, 2 Bramber Road,
London W14 9PB, England

www.johnblakepublishing.co.uk

First published in paperback in 2010

ISBN: 978 1 84454 961 0

British Library Cataloguing-in-Publication Data:

A catalogue record for this book is available from the British Library.

Design by www.envydesign.co.uk

Printed in Great Britain by CPI Bookmarque, Croydon, CR0 4TD

1 3 5 7 9 10 8 6 4 2

© Text copyright Martin Howden 2010

Front cover images and internal photographs reproduced with kind
permission of Rex Features.

Papers used by John Blake Publishing are natural, recyclable products made
from wood grown in sustainable forests. The manufacturing processes conform to
the environmental regulations of the country of origin.

Every attempt has been made to contact the relevant copyright-holders,
but some were unobtainable. We would be grateful if the appropriate
people could contact us.

Contents

Introduction

In the vivid world that Stephenie Meyer has created, vampires do exist. In her imagination, her vampires don't wear cloaks; nor can garlic, crosses or stakes harm them. They can appear outside during the day without fear of burning – while the only visible sign that they are supernatural is their skin, which sparkles when exposed to direct sunlight.

And nor are all of them monsters feasting on human blood.

The Cullen family live in the small US town of Forks in Washington state, residing there in relative peace after striking a truce with the Native American Quileute tribe – who vowed to leave them alone as long as they didn't harm humans or trespass on their land.

But harming humans is something that the Cullen

clan have spent their long lives desperate not to do, anyway. The main reason for that is Carlisle Cullen.

Believing that vampires are a more enhanced version of their human lives, he took the compassion he had from being a mortal doctor into his new life.

After turning into a vampire in the 17th century, he was distraught at what he had become and tried to kill himself many times – attempts that always ended in failure. After finally giving in to his bloodlust and feeding on a passing deer, he realised that he could live off animals without feeding on humans. And so Carlisle decided to do something positive with his transformation, and for centuries he has devoted his life to treating and caring for humans as a doctor.

After a short stint with the vampire coven that is the Volturi – an Italian family who are seen as vampire royalty – he left to travel the world. It was during that time that he ended up fostering several vampire children.

He met the love of his live in the shape of Esme (born in the late 19th century). She first met Carlisle when she was 16 after he treated her broken leg. She ended up in an abusive marriage with a man named Charles Evenson, but, when her son died, the grief-stricken Esme tried to commit suicide by throwing herself off a cliff. Presumed dead, she ended up in the morgue, where Carlisle sensed a faint heartbeat and ended up changing her into a vampire.

Then came Rosalie. In 1915 in New York, Rosalie

Hale was born into a glamorous world of distinction and elegance. Disarmed by her beauty and class, Royce King II proposed to her – and she quickly accepted.

However, after she was beaten up and left to die by her husband and his friends, she was rescued by Carlisle – who transformed her into a vampire. Despite her notorious vanity, she did not appreciate the beauty and immortality offered to her as one of the undead, and would give it all up to be human again and to have children.

Her husband is Emmett, who himself was made into a vampire after he was mauled by a bear in the 1930s. It was Rosalie who found him and took him to Carlisle for the transformation to be carried out.

There is also Alice Cullen. Born Mary Alice Brandon in the early 20th century, she was committed to an asylum because of her ability to see into the future. Despite her troubled beginning, she is a sparky and fun member of the Cullen family who is incredibly close to her brother Edward.

Jasper Hale is another adopted son of the Cullens. The Texan joined the Confederate Army in 1861 during the American Civil War. He was turned into a bloodsucker by a vampire named Maria. He was then given a task of training young vampires and killing them, usually a year later, when they began to outlive their usefulness.

After realising that he could now feel his victims' emotional last moments after a hundred years of working with Maria, he decided be could no longer feast on human flesh. Luckily for him, he met Alice (who had had visions of meeting him that day) and together they went out to find the Cullen family in the hope that they might live their lives in peace and without killing humans.

And then there is Edward Cullen, born in 1901. He was changed by Carlisle in his late teens after his mother begged the doctor to save her son when he was dying of Spanish flu.

Like the rest of the Cullen family, they drink only animal blood. Believing their lives as vampires are as safe as can be, they are a happy and loving family.

This is the story of the actors who play one of the most memorable vampire families alive – or is that dead?

chapter one

Robert's
Early Years

'We have lots of lovely boys here but he was something special.'
— Tower House School Secretary, Caroline Booth

Robert Pattinson is someone who hides away from the media glare as much as possible and generally favours low-budget art-house fare over mainstream blockbusters. So how did he become one of Hollywood's most recognisable faces and brightest talents?

The fact that he did so while never shirking from his ideals, always making sure his performances were not what anyone was expecting, makes his rise even more extraordinary.

This strength in belief comes from his parents, Clare and Richard, and is shown not only in him, but his two older sisters, Elizabeth and Victoria.

Robert Thomas Pattinson was born in London on 13 May 1986 at a private hospital in Barnes, London, the area where he would enjoy a loving and happy childhood. Barnes is an affluent riverside suburb, its many elegant and luxurious 19th-century buildings being proof of its high-end reputation.

Despite this, Pattinson was brought up with a strong work ethic – something that was instilled in him from a young age. While his parents were well off financially through his father's job importing vintage cars from America and his mother's work as a booker at a modelling agency, he and his two sisters were never spoilt – with their parents ensuring that they knew the value of money by making sure they would earn their keep themselves. In Pattinson's case this was a regular early-morning paper round.

Clare and Richard also ensured that their children were well educated in politics and the arts. However, he jokingly concedes that he struggles to be up to date on current affairs now because of both the time factor and the fact that he's now in the showbiz world – conceding that he knows more about Miley Cyrus's public life than he does about today's politics.

However, his aunt, Diana Nutley, says he 'was brought up very modestly' – and that it was far from a strongly disciplined household.

'Rob got his quirky sense of humour from his father,' she recalled. 'They are a very close-knit middle-class family.'

Richard and London-born Clare met in a pub in Surrey through a friend in common when she was 26 and he 35 – and the pair quickly agreed on the way they would raise their three children. As we have seen, they would not spoil them, preferring instead to let them choose their own path.

Robert was incredibly close to his older sisters – both at a young age and into his adult life – save the occasional teasing he had to endure from them. 'I was twelve, my sisters used to dress me up as a girl and introduce me as "Claudia!",' Pattinson explained.

He has been described as being somewhat 'arty' and 'bohemian'. So it shouldn't come as much surprise that his education at two posh private schools isn't looked on with fond memories from the actor.

From 1992 to 1998, he attended Tower House School, a prep school for boys.

Pattinson then went to the Harrodian School, which taught both male and female students. Even at a young age, the roguish Pattinson was very happy to be attending a mixed school.

'Twelve was a turning point, as I moved to a mixed school, and then I became cool and discovered hair gel,' he said, with a twinkle in his eye. Incidentally, twelve was the age that Pattinson had his first kiss.

With Pattinson's face now adorning many a young girl's bedroom walls, it should come as no surprise that he was something of a heartthrob. Pupils who went to his school remember how he would at times sit by himself during lunch breaks with a book in his hand.

'I was quite shy,' Pattinson has said. However, his

Aunt Diana remembered that 'he had lots of friends, but he didn't date much'.

Tower House school secretary Caroline Booth said he was one of their prized students, 'He was an absolutely lovely boy; everyone adored him. We have lots of lovely boys here but he was something special. He was very pretty, beautiful and blonde.'

Both schools are establishments that prided themselves on academic excellence – with Harrodian urging the students that 'good manners and consideration for others are expected and European and global awareness promoted'.

It was a rigid and strict environment that wasn't best suited to his outlook on life – which seemed to hinge on soaking up art and culture rather than learning about dry academic subjects. As for the school's insistence that Pattinson should be 'confident in French', he remarked, 'I speak French, sort of. At, like, a three-year-old's standard.'

It wasn't all a loss, however.

'My favourite teacher was probably my English teacher, because she got me into writing instead of just answering the question. I used to hand in homework with twenty pages of nonsense and she'd still mark it. She was a really amazing teacher.'

The other classes didn't do it for the young Pattinson, as his Aunt Diana explained. 'He was hopelessly lazy. He didn't really study very hard.'

Pattinson agreed, saying, 'I wasn't very academic.

My school reports were always pretty bad. I never ever did homework. I always turned up for lessons, as I liked my teachers, but my report said I didn't try very hard.'

When Pattinson did take the studies seriously, he normally excelled himself – but those times were few and far between. It was only when his like-minded friends all competed with each other when something took their fancy that they put their all into their studies.

'The few times that we decided to do homework we'd just be competing with each other. If it was an English essay or something, we wouldn't do 90 per cent of the homework, and then something would come along with an interesting title and we'd all do, like, a thesis on it just to beat each other. I've kind of grown up around really competitive, artistic-type people, luckily, and I'm very, very grateful for that as well,' he told the US magazine *Life Story*.

It wasn't that Robert was necessarily an unruly student – although he did win the Untidy Desk Award in 1998 – nor was he mischievous. It was just that he preferred to daydream in class rather than study. And he would take that trait into his career. A Pattinson film set wouldn't be a Pattinson film set without the actor lazing around between takes, deep in isolated thought or with a book in his hand.

With Pattinson not exactly setting the education system alight, and the term fees at Harrodian costing just over £4,000, it's perhaps understandable that his dad was having concerns about him staying at the school. Robert's cunning plan to placate his father, however, was to ensure that when his dad indicated that he wanted a word with his son, he would be showcasing his piano skills!

However, according to Pattinson, his dad did finally tell his son, 'OK, you might as well leave, since you're not working very hard.'

His other aunt, Monica Weller, continued the story: 'His dad said he'd have to pay his own fees, then he'd pay him back if he got good grades. So Rob modelled to pay for school [at Harrodian]. And he got an A and two Bs. Rob has got good values and a strong work ethic.

'His career has evolved very quickly – he was in the right place at the right time. We're all hugely proud of him.'

Looking back now, Pattinson concedes that he should have concentrated harder at school: 'I wasn't focused on school and I didn't achieve much. I remember that now, and I always try to remind myself not to waste a moment of life. If I could have done one thing differently, I think it would have been that I would have taken school more seriously.'

As his Aunt Monica said, Robert did indeed try his hand at modelling while he was at school. His first job was delivering newspapers and magazines – and his next one saw him appearing in them!

Given his mother's knowledge of the modelling

industry, some might have accused her of pulling favours to get her son a job – but Pattinson's striking looks and easygoing charisma were always going to have modelling scouts banging at his door, no matter what.

He quickly landed himself a series of jobs, including photoshoots for teen magazines.

Robert remembered, 'I was modelling at twelve, the youngest person in my agency out of the girls or boys. I was so ridiculously skinny I looked like a girl, but that was the period when they loved androgynous-looking people.

'Then, I guess, I became too much of a guy, so I never got any more jobs. I had the most unsuccessful modelling career.'

Models who worked alongside him remember Pattinson as quite shy and nervous. His film career, however, was going to be much more successful and fulfilling than his modelling, but that was such a long way away in Rob's mind. He hadn't been fully bitten by the acting bug yet, but, just as he felt he was coming to a crossroads in life, fate, or more importantly a group of good-looking girls, stepped in.

chapter two

An Actor's Life for Me

'I remember he was verrrrrry handsome!'
– Rob's *Vanity Fair* co-star Reese Witherspoon

Despite the plaudits he would earn for his performances in later roles, Pattinson's first break into acting was the result of his eye for a lady – or ladies in this case.

He and his dad were in a restaurant when the young Pattinson spied a group of young ladies. To Robert's amazement, his dad went over to them and asked where they had been. Elaborating on this conversation, Pattinson explained, 'They said they went to this drama club and he says, "Rob, you've got to go down to this club." That's the only time he's done anything like that. It was just the weirdest thing, and he had nagged me about attending. At one point he said he would pay me, which is pretty strange. I don't know what his intentions were.'

Robert's intentions weren't exactly honourable; he's admitted that he attended only because 'lots of pretty girls went there'.

Both Tower House and Harrodian school had excellent drama facilities, with the former stating that their drama club would help students 'gain invaluable experience in performing in front of people in a relaxed, uninhibited environment' – while Harrodian boasted 'first-rate drama productions, art exhibitions and musical events'.

School secretary Booth remembers, 'I wouldn't say he was a star, but he was very keen on our drama club, I do remember that.'

However, despite these first-rate facilities and an early acting role when Pattinson was six, in a play called *Spell for a Rhyme* at Tower House, and a role in an amateur production of the *Lord of the Flies*, it was actually Barnes Theatre Company that helped transform the young man into the actor he has now become.

He started out backstage for a while, helping out with the technical side of stage productions. But a spur-of-the-moment decision to audition for *Guys and Dolls* paid dividends: it resulted in his getting a 'tiny part or something' in the production.

What he learnt straightaway was the pure release he got when performing. While some go into their shell when having to perform, some latch onto the experience with relish. He was very much the latter, even at this early stage.

He would take a bigger leap in the next theatre production – *Our Town* – by bagging the lead part.

Luckily for Pattinson, he was spotted by an agent fairly quickly. His performances may not have been note perfect but his raw and vibrant acting impressed the agent. Buoyed by confidence, he went on to bag a role in a stage production of *Macbeth* for the Old Sorting Office – an arts charitable trust based in Barnes, which helps nurture young acting talents.

And it was to get even better for the fledgling actor. He landed a role in 2004's lavish film adaptation of *Vanity Fair*, which was based on the 18th-century satirical comedy by William Makepeace Thackeray.

Directed by Mira Nair, the film sees Reese Witherspoon play a young woman called Becky Sharp, who attempts to climb all the way up the social ladder.

It was a dream come true for Pattinson, who would play Sharp's son – although he would concede that playing the 'son' of Witherspoon, who was only 10 years older than he was, was 'ridiculous'.

In what would be a regular occurrence, Pattinson wasn't sure that he deserved to be in such surroundings. He remembered, 'You have a trailers and stuff. It was the most ridiculous thing. And I was thinking, "I shouldn't be an actor. I'm doing a movie with Reese Witherspoon. How is this happening?"'

And his confidence was going to a take a further battering when he turned up to the screening of the film with his actor pal Tom Sturridge (who also had a part in the movie).

Unfortunately for Pattinson, no one had told him that his scenes had been cut.

He told *Vanity Fair* magazine, 'We had scenes right next to each other and it was both our first jobs. We went to the screening; we thought the whole thing was such a joke anyway, because we had no idea what we were doing. We were, like, "acting" or whatever – we had no idea – and we watched [Sturridge's] scene and were like, "Yeah, that's pretty good, that's all right."'

But then came the moment that every actor dreads.

'I'm sitting there going, "Ummmm... really?" No one had told me that I had been cut out.'

While his scenes can now be seen on the DVD release of the film, it was a crushing moment for the young actor.

Nonetheless, the Oscar-winning actress recalled her moments with Pattinson, saying, 'I remember he was verrrrrry handsome! I was like, "I have a really handsome son." I had to sob and cry all over him, but he was great.'

Disappointed he may have been, but Pattinson would quickly get another chance to make an impression in front of the camera. He signed on to star in the fantasy epic *Ring of the Nibelungs*, a film and TV miniseries based on Norse mythology. But this was more than just a chance for the young actor to prove himself. Because the film was shot in Africa, he was to stay there by himself. For an independent free spirit, it was a once-in-a-lifetime opportunity.

Unfortunately, because the shoot coincided with his final school exams, he had to juggle a harsh study time with his strict filming schedule. He still managed to achieve an A and two Bs, but, as ever, Pattinson wasn't easy to please.

'I don't know how that happened. I didn't even know half the syllabus. I lost faith in the exam system at that point,' he said.

While *Ring of the Nibelungs* failed to make an impression, his next film role was to be a far more successful one. He signed on to play Cedric Diggory in the fourth *Harry Potter* film – the most successful franchise in cinema history. And this was down to the fact that the casting director on *Vanity Fair*, Fiona Weir, was the same one on *Harry Potter and the Goblet of Fire*.

In fact, if you believe Pattinson, he was picked only because the casting agent felt guilty about his being cut out of *Vanity Fair*. However, it's fair to say that the plum role of Cedric Diggory would never have been cast just out of guilt.

Talking about his character, Pattinson said, 'Cedric is competitive, but he's also a nice guy who plays fair and sticks to the rules. I sort of identify with Cedric in a couple of ways. I'm not as nice as he is: he tends to do the right thing all the time and I never feel the need to do that. I think he's a pretty cool character.'

The film's director, Mike Newell, explained, 'Cedric exemplifies all that you would expect the [wizarding academy] Hogwarts champion to be. Robert Pattinson was born to play the role – he's quintessentially English with chiselled public-schoolboy good looks.'

With a cast that included the likes of Sir Michael Gambon, Timothy Spall, Jason Isaacs, Dame Maggie Smith, Alan Rickman and Ralph Fiennes, he was desperate to soak up and learn from the collective experience on set.

At the start of the shoot, he would be so overcome with nerves that he would start throwing up. As time went by his confidence and stature grew, and he began to realise he belonged in such an environment. In fact, he began to enjoy it so much that he feared for his character's death scene late on in the movie – envious that the other actors had 'another three films guaranteed'.

Pattinson did come back in a cameo flashback sequence in *Harry Potter and the Order of the Phoenix*, but his time in the franchise was essentially over.

It was a life-changing experience, however. Not only did he get to act with some of the finest British actors the country has produced, but he also got his first taste of fame.

Speaking shortly before the film was released, he said, 'Somebody asked me for my autograph the other day. Because I finished school and I'm not really doing anything at the moment, I was just kind of aimlessly wandering around London, and these two guys who were about thirty came up and asked for my autograph. I was really quite proud at the time, and they wanted to take photos and stuff.

'I've been to a couple of Warner Bros premieres in the last few weeks and, considering no one knows who I am, it's still a pretty scary event. So I don't know what it's gonna be like when you actually have to do something rather than just walk in. I still trip over my feet and stuff when I'm not supposed to do be doing anything. So, I'll just see how it goes. I'm looking forward to it.'

He now concedes he never handled the fame side of it well during that time: 'I've changed so much. I'm not nearly as cocky as I was. I was a real prat for the first month. I didn't talk to anyone.'

But at that moment, following his breakout performance in *Goblet of Fire*, it seemed the new heartthrob had the world in his hands. However, when everyone expected Robert to go one way, he went the other. Rather than cement his status as the Next Big Thing by appearing in a soulless blockbuster, he preferred to make left-field choices that would improve his acting talents rather than his bank balance.

Renting a 'cool little ex-crack den' in Soho with his childhood pals Tom Sturridge and Sam Bradley, he spent time relaxing with them and playing music. It was a period that Robert describes as 'the best time I ever had'.

'We spent the better part of a year just getting drunk

every night. [The flat] was so cool. You had to walk through a restaurant kitchen to get up to the roofs, but you could walk along all the roofs. I didn't do anything for a year – I just sat on the roof and played music.'

Bradley, who would end up co-writing the song 'Never Think' with Pattinson – which featured in *Twilight* – remembered that it 'was a creative environment with not much furniture and a TV with a PlayStation'.

'It was cool. I think about that place every day,' he added.

Pattinson did eventually land another job however, and it was not the one expected of a rising star. He signed on for an obscure play called *The Woman Before* alongside *Friends* actress Helen Baxendale. For Pattinson, it was a dream job – and made perfect sense for the rookie actor. Determined to avoid becoming just another pretty-boy player churned out by the Hollywood system, he wanted roles that appealed to him and ones that would make him a better actor. However, his dream job would quickly turn out to be a nightmare after he was sacked from the play.

It was a cruel blow, and only now does he readily admit why he was axed.

He was at first bullish about his exit, saying, 'I liked the freedom and the things you could do with acting. Like if you want to look sad, you don't have to have a sad face, which is still how I try on a lot of different things. For that same reason – trying to take risks – I got fired from that play. I haven't really changed since I got fired.

'It's probably one of the best things that ever happened to me. I got some jobs afterward, by saying I got fired and for standing up for what I believe in.'

However, he now candidly admits that it was a case of trying too hard: 'I thought I was doing something interesting, and I ended up getting fired for it. I think I just got confused, doing random mannerisms, as if that made an interesting performance. I was going to all these auditions and telling everyone how I got fired because I stood up for my principles, and making up all this bullshit.'

Disappointed, he went 'kind of nuts for a while'.

He stopped taking calls from his agent, and, with the involvement of his pals, instead threw himself back into his music. They played impromptu gigs, with Pattinson happily jamming away with his fellow talented musicians. There were also times when Pattinson performed solo.

It was a bittersweet time for him because, while he was hugely enjoying himself doing what he loved, and, more importantly, doing things by himself (no countless auditions and heartbreaking disappointments here), there was still a nagging sadness that he hadn't achieved what he wanted with his acting career.

He would have a chance to make amends in the British TV movie *The Haunted Airman* – and it was a role that showcased his quirky talents immediately.

Based on the novel *The Haunting of Toby Jugg* by the occult writer Dennis Wheatley, the story concerns a flight lieutenant (Pattinson) who, after being wounded during World War Two, moves to a remote Welsh mansion. It's in these surroundings that things take a turn for the worse, when he begins to suffer terrifying visions.

The Haunted Airman also gave Robert a chance to team up once more with Julian Sands, who starred in *Ring of the Nibelungs*. Sands played the creepy psychiatrist who examines him.

The *Stage* described the film as 'a disturbing, beautifully made and satisfyingly chilling ghost story'. Pattinson himself was singled out for praise, with his performance earning rave reviews for his 'perfect combination of youthful terror and world-weary cynicism'.

For Pattinson, it was just the second wind that he needed. It gave him huge confidence and the belief that he did have the ability needed to make a name for himself in front of the camera.

'It just changed my whole opinion about everything.'

Next up was a role alongside the British comedian and actress Catherine Tate in another British TV movie, *The Bad Mother's Handbook*. It was yet another film based on a novel (nearly all of Pattinson's film roles are) – in this case by Kate Long.

He played a nerdy student who has a crush on Tate's character's daughter in the charming comedy. It showed the usually dramatic actor in a more comedic light, highlighting his versatile talents.

There is something of a stubborn streak in Pattinson's personality. After his high-profile exit from *The Woman Before* over his attempts to experiment with his character, other actors would have shied away from such things in later roles. But, if anything, it made him seek even more offbeat and alternative roles – and, even if the character wasn't written like that, he would do everything he could to locate it (something he would tap into for Edward Cullen).

First-time director Oliver Irving recalled Pattinson's audition for the charming comedy film *How To Be*: 'Robert walked into the audition and reminded me of people I know. I think he forgot his lines and just started improvising, which is exactly what I wanted – someone who could just become the character and leave the kind of "techniques" they train in at drama schools. I had a hunch he would do well with [the] other cast.

'He's a really down-to-earth guy – it was funny because he told us he had a part in a *Harry Potter*, but, as you can imagine, many actors in England have had tiny parts in those films. Plus, he really underplayed it, so I didn't think much of it at the time. It wasn't until we had cast him, that I watched the *Harry Potter* film he was in and realised he had a major part.'

How To Be tells the story of a loner called Art, a singer/songwriter who is struggling to cope with life's hardships. After his girlfriend dumps him, he moves back home – with quirky consequences.

Determined to prove his acting chops, Pattinson would, remarked Irving, 'make his eyes water and get himself all worked up, slapping himself and doing everything he possibly could to make him feel ill' during a dramatic scene in the film.

How To Be would tirelessly work its way through the festival circuit in its initial bid to get distribution. But it's found a second life, thanks to Pattinson's *Twilight* success – and the actor couldn't be happier.

'*Twilight* is helping. I went to Austin festival and it was packed because of *Twilight*. I loved the script. I loved the ending. No one claps and he doesn't even notice. I thought that was such a feel-good ending, even though it's not really.'

Irving was obviously grateful for Robert's newly found A-list status, adding, 'Every so often someone will love the movie and never have even really heard of Rob. But, then, often people will say, "I came because of Rob but I loved this film in its own right."'

While he was buoyed by the reaction of his last few performances – and with confidence levels rising from each subsequent film – he didn't want to rest on his laurels. Luckily for him, his next project would be his toughest one yet.

Little Ashes – a biopic of the famous surrealist painter Salvador Dalí – was something that Pattinson had been circling around for two years.

Born in 1904, Salvador Domingo Felipe Jacinto Dalí is seen as the most famous of the artists during the surrealist era. But it was Dalí's younger years, when he met the poet Federico García Lorca, that would be the main focus of the film.

The part of Dalí was a plum role for any actor – never mind a young one still finding his feet. But, in the beginning, Pattinson was originally going to play the other lead part in the film – that of Lorca, the homosexual poet who embarked on a passionate relationship with Dalí.

He revealed, 'It took ages to get this film made. It was a really interesting script, and, about a year after I was in mind for Lorca, I read for Dalí, and about a year after that they suddenly said, "Oh, we've got money, we're doing it in Spain and it starts in four days." So I came and just thought it would be kind of fun – I mean, you know, the stuff Dalí makes, kind of crazy – and I thought it would be quite fun to do.'

While it would be an incredibly satisfying job for Pattinson, it certainly wasn't fun.

'I wanted to have a vacation in Spain,' he said. 'But it became just – really, really hard. I'd never done a job that was so hard.'

While the logistics of shooting in an environment where most of the crew spoke a language that he didn't speak (Spanish) were tough, the biggest sources of hardship on the film were down to Pattinson himself. Typically, he didn't make things easy for himself.

Becoming so determined to immerse himself fully in the role, he stripped away any inhibitions he once had. Throwing himself completely into the role, he pored over hours and hours of research, trawling through the many contradictions that surround the playful and complex Dalí in a bid to find a true voice for the role.

The film was shot before, but released after, *Twilight*, and most of the media attention was focused on Pattinson's homosexual love scenes rather than the film itself – although it has to be said that it was Pattinson's fame that thrust the film into the limelight.

Talking about the risk that the film would be overshadowed by Robert's gay and nude scenes, British actor Matthew McNulty, who plays director Luis Buñuel in the film, remarked during the movie's promotion, 'Possibly, to people that haven't seen the film, but I'm not really bothered about that. If people want to judge it before they've actually seen it and judge it on the fact that there's a teen heartthrob playing the lead, then that's more fool them. I think that the film has got merit of its own through its writing and the cinematography. Hopefully, word of mouth will dispel any of that.'

The *Hollywood Reporter* wasn't completely smitten by the film, although it did concede that it was 'often enjoyable to watch' and reserved praise for Pattinson's performance, saying he 'captures the initial shyness and growing flamboyance of Dalí'.

Acclaimed film critic Roger Ebert said, 'Little Ashes is absorbing but not compelling'.

The Guardian, however, said that Robert 'struggles to portray the hugely complex Dalí with any real conviction'.

Overall, though, it was a success for Robert – both professionally and personally. Career-wise it was a left-field choice, but ultimately a bold one. More importantly, however, it was also a role that erased any remaining doubts that he had over his ability as an actor. He put so much into the part that he became the character. It made him realise that acting was definitely the job for him. He now had the ability to be a chameleon playing different kinds of roles.

Ironically, he wasn't to know it, but just as he was beginning to think about carving a career out of playing left-field characters, he was going to sink his teeth into his biggest and most mainstream role yet – that of Edward Cullen.

But, before we find out how he landed the role of a lifetime, we'll take a look at the early lives of the other actors who make up the Cullen clan.

chapter three
The Father Figure

'I kind of look to my own parents for inspiration. They've been together their whole marriage, and they raised a great family; my sisters and I are very close.' – Peter Facinelli

Facinelli was ten years old when he knew he was going to be an actor. 'I know where I'm going. I've just been waiting for everyone to catch up,' he would say. However, at ten years old, growing up in a somewhat traditional household with dreams of being an actor, was like 'telling my parents I wanted to go to the moon'.

Born on 26 November 1973 to Italian immigrants, he grew up 'in the middle of nowhere in Queens'. It was a house primarily filled with women. With his dad Pierino (or Peter Sr, as he is also known) working sometimes up to six days a week, Peter Jr would generally be the only male in a household that included his mother Bruna, his three sisters Jo, Lisa and Linda, and his grandmother. It was a household situation that would eventually be replicated with his own family.

Talking about his childhood in Ozone Park, he remembered, 'Queens was a great neighbourhood to grow up in because, at the time, you could go out and ride your bike on the street without your mom having to worry. My neighbourhood was on the Brooklyn–Queens border, sandwiched between two cultures (Cubans and Italians). That was pretty fantastic. To this day, some of my best friends are those Cuban kids I grew up with.'

It was a household filled with love and laughter – and he would always look at his parents' relationship as an ideal template for a long-lasting marriage.

'I kind of look to my own parents for inspiration. They've been together their whole marriage, and they raised a great family; my sisters and I are very close.'

There were also strict moral standards that he would have to adhere to, however.

In an interview with *Contents* magazine, he jokingly revealed, 'I wasn't allowed to watch *The Love Boat* because my grandmother would stand downstairs and yell at me because women were walking around in bikinis.

'She would get magazines in the mail and cut out all the sexy pictures and throw them out. I didn't kiss a girl until I was about sixteen. I threw rocks at them until I was about fifteen because I didn't want my sisters to tease me.'

It was the unlikely location of a library at St Francis Preparatory High School that would sow the acting seeds in Facinelli's mind. He came across a book on *Butch Cassidy and the Sundance Kid* – which featured the actors Paul Newman and Robert Redford on the cover.

He said, 'And I thought they were the coolest guys in the world. I hadn't seen the movie, so I went and saw it, and that was it for me.'

Despite his longing to be an actor, he never pursued it at high school, preferring to skip classes occasionally to shoot some pool instead. At the time he was just too shy and lacking in confidence to get up in front of his classmates and act.

He remembered, 'I just hated high school. It was two hours away and I had to take four buses to get there. There were a lot [of] cliques and I didn't want to be labelled. It's kinda like Hollywood. But I miss it, the simplicity of it. You thought life was stressful because you got a pimple on your face and you didn't want to go to school.'

While he had dreams of being an actor, it wasn't the stage that he saw as his future. Obsessed with movies, he was desperate to appear on the screen. As a teenager and into his twenties he would 'rent a movie about every night'.

Acting was to take a backseat, however, because, to the delight of his parents, he decided to attend St John's University to study pre-law. 'It seemed to impress people in my family when I said, "I want to be a lawyer when I grow up."' Whenever he told them he wanted to be an actor, they 'all looked at me like I had five heads'.

However, working as an intern with a Manhattan law film confirmed that that sort of career was not for him. '[They] spent most of their time sitting in little cubicle offices,' he remembered. 'I realised that lawyers spend most of their time trying not to go to court. They told me that court was the last place you want to be. So I threw away the courtroom drama and just went straight for the drama, and I transferred to NYU [New York University]. I told my parents, "To be a good lawyer, I have to be a good actor, so I'm going to take acting classes at NYU and study theatre there." And they bought it. And then I started working, right out of NYU. So, when my parents realised it was something that I could do, they were behind it.'

At NYU, he was extremely happy to hone his talents. He revelled in the environment, learning new techniques and skills.

'It's all kind of bizarre. I mean there's no right way to do it. I studied a couple of different techniques. You have [Sanford] Meisner on one side of the scale, which is very moment acting – I studied Meisner, which the Atlantic Theater Company taught at NYU – and then there's [Lee] Strasberg, which is very method, where you search within your life to find the character. It's the difference between internal and external. At PAW,

Practical Aesthetic Workshop, you have this character that you create. You don't believe you're the character. The character is completely external – the way you walk, the way you talk.'

Despite enjoying the time at NYU, he would leave 15 credits shy of graduating, after landing a role in the 1995 film *Angela*.

Banking $150 from the film, he proudly showed his dad that he could make a living from acting.

'When I brought home a paycheque for my first job, my dad's like, "He got a paycheque; maybe he can make a living out of it."'

However, it was only until fairly recently that his father was still telling him that he had a room back at theirs whenever he needed it.

'I'm like, "Dad, I have a wife and two kids – I'm not going to be moving back into the house, hopefully." '

Despite his dad's jesting, Facinelli is one of the lucky actors: ever since he decided to be a professional actor he has managed to work steadily, avoiding being a waiter or a barman to earn some cash while waiting for a big break.

He told *Teen Hollywood*, 'I don't think I ever thought I wouldn't make a living or a career out of it. I never had a backup plan. For me, it was always a do-or-die kind of thing. When people ask me if there's any advice that I'd give them, I say, "Don't have a backup plan 'cause you'll use it." I didn't have a backup plan. I started working out of college, and I just went from job to job and never looked back. I always made my living, from that point on, as an actor. I never thought that I wouldn't.

'I've been lucky that I haven't had to take jobs outside of acting. So far acting has been my main provider,' he said. When it wasn't acting, he would briefly hold down a career as a model.

He proclaimed himself one to watch in a 1995 episode of the enduring US TV show *Law & Order*, in which he played a teen rapist. He would earn further plaudits playing a male hustler in *The Price of Love*.

It was his next project that would have a huge impact on his life. And it wasn't about his career. During filming of the TV movie *An Unfinished Affair*, he met *Beverly Hills 90210* star Jennie Garth, who was in the middle of divorcing her first husband. They would fall in love, and Garth would fall pregnant within a year – a situation that could have been fraught with family drama, given Facinelli's Catholic upbringing. She told *People*, 'This was a big deal for him and his family to have a baby out of wedlock. But he said, "I'm not going to let them pressure me. We took a good four years to strengthen the foundation of our relationship."'

Facinelli added, 'I didn't want to get married just because we had a kid. I didn't feel like that was fair to anybody. When we [finally] got married there was no nervousness.'

After he proposed by spreading Hershey's Kisses

chocolates on the bed with a ring hidden inside one of the wrappers, they finally tied the knot in 2001, and both couldn't be happier still. Garth would say, 'It's like winning an Oscar, it's huge. We don't take it for granted.'

And, with his family life blossoming, so did his acting career.

His big break came in 1998 – starring with a-then big box office draw, Jennifer Love Hewitt. *Can't Hardly Wait* was a teen romantic comedy, very much in the vein of eighties high-school films. Facinelli played the jock in the film, who dumps Love Hewitt's character.

Much was expected from *Can't Hardly Wait*, but it sank at the box office – perhaps weighed down by the generally negative reviews. It did thrust Facinelli into the spotlight, however, but it was nothing compared with what his younger *Twilight* stars have had to put up with.

'Things were different then: we were young, and in the movie teens were watching but, there [weren't] paparazzi out taking all of our pictures. Now, thirty seconds after a picture is taken, it's on the Internet; and, forty-five seconds later, hundreds of people have commented on it.'

He went on to star in *Telling You* and *Welcome to Hollywood*, before he was given a huge chance to impress in 1999's *The Big Kahuna*, where he would go toe to toe with acting heavyweights Kevin Spacey and Danny DeVito.

Shot just under three weeks, *The Big Kahuna* tells the story of three men trying to win a pitch at a sales convention. Facinelli told *Interview* magazine, 'It was a challenging part because you're in a room with these two older, experienced guys and you don't want to get steamrolled by them. I just tried to play the character as truthfully as I could.'

In fact, Spacey, who was producing, had seen Facinelli in a number of things, had been impressed by what he saw and put the actor on a shortlist to show the film's director John Swanbeck.

Facinelli remembered, 'Kevin is just a great person, a great actor. Very humble. He's directed before and he produced *The Big Kahuna*, so he could have easily come in and said this is how we're going to do it, but he didn't. He came in and made everybody feel like an equal. I was just as equal as Danny DeVito and Kevin, and it was so beautiful and inspiring.'

While the film itself feels more suited to the theatre than the cinema, the performances were praised, with *Variety* stating, 'Newcomer Facinelli, who looks very much like the young Tom Cruise, holds his own in a demanding role full of surprise.'

It wouldn't be the first time that he would be labelled the next Tom Cruise, but, as time has gone by in his career it's a tag that has, to his great relief, begun to disappear.

The British gangster flick *Honest* provided another film role of note, which marked the film debuts of the then popular girl group All Saints. He would be the only real American actor in the movie, and jokingly conceded that he was there only because they 'needed some dumb American in the movie to slap around'.

Big things were definitely expected of the sci-fi action film *Supernova*, which he starred in alongside James Spader and Angela Bassett. But several problems behind the scenes didn't help (it went through several directors), and it ended up with savage reviews and poor box office takings.

Romper Stomper director Geoffrey Wright was originally attached to the project but was let go, leaving veteran director Walter Hill to take control. However, the studio weren't happy with his cut of the film and instead turned to Oscar-winning filmmaker Francis Ford Coppola:

'When we started the project, it was an interesting movie. It didn't exactly come out to be that,' rued Facinelli. 'But I think there were pieces missing that didn't allow the audience to get what Walter Hill had really set out to do. But that's not Walter's fault. There were a lot of changes in the film and Walter wanted to do some reshoots, but they wouldn't allow it. So other directors took it over and then put it together. Coppola then ended up doing the final cut. He did a great job putting it together but when you don't have all the pieces the story ends up not being clear.'

At the end of the day, Facinelli thought it was 'a good film but I didn't think it was a great film'.

Film Comment wrote an astute article entitled 'When Worlds Collide – What Francis Coppola did to Walter Hill's superb sci-fi film *Supernova* explodes the myth of filmmakers looking out for one another'.

In the piece, journalist Gregory Solman wrote, 'Coppola's cruelest cuts eviscerate Hill's action direction. Somebody had to finish the movie but getting Coppola to improve Hill's action is trading one director's proven strength for another's historic weakness.'

The film's original director, Wright, told the horror film magazine *Fangoria*, 'I think that they were looking for a pilot for a television series. They were spending a lot of money on this movie, and they wanted something to rival *Star Trek*. I was not interested in doing a pilot for a television series.'

While Facinelli was still looking for his breakout hit, he could at least be proud that roles such as that of the jock in *Can't Hardly Wait*, the salesman in *Big Kahuna* and the villain in *Supernova* resulted in varied performances.

'The biggest compliment I get sometimes is, "I didn't even know that was you," which makes it harder because Hollywood wants to label you to sell you,' he has said.

Despite scoring roles in *Rennie's Landing*, *Tempting*, the Drew Barrymore comedy *Riding in Cars with Boys* and the action blockbuster *The Scorpion King*, he was becoming frustrated. He remarked at the time, 'Sometimes I wish I was in a different place. I've done eleven films in four and a half years, so I've been working a lot. I've seen people who have done two movies, and all of a sudden they're on the covers of magazines. I think, "Well, how come I've done eleven films and I'm not on any magazine?" But I'm actually happy because I'm not in this industry to rise to the top in two weeks and then fall in a year.'

He had begun to start a family, and was desperate to be there with them as much as possible. While his long-term goal was still to conquer the big screen, an opportunity presented itself in the form of the small screen.

Since Facinelli was not a 'TV snob', he was more than happy to star in a TV series, which also provided some stability and ensured that he was close to home. It was *Fastlane* – a *Miami Vice*-type show, which starred Facinelli as a maverick undercover cop alongside Bill Bellamy as his partner.

Noting that the script had the same sort of funny buddy elements that featured in the film that kick-started his dream to be an actor – *Butch Cassidy and the Sundance Kid* – he was hugely excited about getting to work on the show. All he had to do was complete a screen test. He was confident and raring to go, but a day before he was due to test for the role the show's bosses put it back a week. Luckily, he managed to get over that disappointment, and bagged the role when he finally got to show them what he was capable of.

It was hardly high art, but it was a fun role – albeit

a very physical one. 'If I don't go home without a cut or a bruise, I don't feel like I put in a good day. I still [have] a scar from the cut I got going over that hood [in the series pilot]; half my body was left on the hood.'

As he says, 'You don't want to be in a baseball game and not play.'

Tagged as a 'guilty pleasure', Facinelli had no problem with that description. 'Hey,' he said. 'Godiva chocolates are a guilty pleasure, too, and I'll take Godiva chocolates whenever I can get them. Bill said it best: "We're like the pretty girl with the ugly feet." People don't want to like us, but they don't want to say they don't like us [either], because there's nothing like us on TV.'

Produced by *Charlie's Angels* director McG (Joseph McGinty Nichol), *Fastlane* was a racy show that would feature Facinelli in regular clinches with beautiful Hollywood actresses – something that he and his wife felt uncomfortable with. 'It's definitely awkward,' he told *People* magazine.

'I watch the show, but I've learned that it's best not to watch the love scenes,' admitted Garth. 'We have such a strong bond that it's really hard to watch his body doing those scenes.'

He knew that a large appeal of the show was that it was beautiful people playing action heroes – and he had no problem making sure he kept his toned physique. As one magazine put it, 'He's out of his clothes so often you'd think the series didn't have a costume budget.'

'I want to look good,' Facinelli added. 'Why let yourself go and be eating tons of doughnuts at the craft service table? I think there is a certain responsibility. I don't mind showing my ass on film. Everyone's got a backside – some are hairier than others, you know?'

Garth's former *Beverly Hills 90210* co-star Tiffani-Amber Thiessen (now credited as just Tiffani Thiessen) would play his boss. Facinelli was friends with Thiessen before they worked on *Fastlane* because of the connections they both had to Garth, describing her as 'like my sister'.

Garth insists the cocky, tough-guy persona seen in the show is just Hollywood magic: 'He doesn't watch football or sports; he doesn't drink beer. He's not a guy's guy in that respect.'

Thiessen agreed, saying, 'He's a big old geek. He's a woman, too! He's got this sensitivity about him. He's like having a girlfriend around.'

Weirdly enough, on US TV Facinelli's *Fastlane* would air on Fox at the same time on a Friday night as Garth's Warner Bros sitcom *What I like About You*. Garth told *TV Guide*, 'If we were on shows that were similar, it would be harder. But he'll have an episode about drug heists or counterfeiting and mine will be about a lost teddy bear.

'I wasn't very happy at first because no one wants to be up against their spouse. I don't know what we'd do if we were both home on Friday nights. We'd probably fight over it [the remote].'

Sadly, *Fastlane* ran for only 22 episodes, and was axed because of low ratings and high production costs.

It wasn't the end of Facinelli on the small screen, however, as he bagged himself a recurring role in the critically acclaimed HBO show *Six Feet Under*, where he played one of the character Claire's art-school friends.

Several small-scale films followed, including *Finding Amanda* and the lead role in 2006's *Hollow Man 2*. The direct-to-DVD sequel to *Hollow Man* sees Facinelli play Frank Turner, a detective assigned to investigate a strange murder. In doing so he stumbles upon a top-secret military operation involving invisible soldiers.

It was not well received, with one review saying, 'This is about as needless and pointless as a sequel as they come.'

In 2007, he also excelled in the first season of *Damages*, in which he played Gregory Malina. This was a seemingly small-time player in the legal TV series, which stars Glen Close, but it turns out he is one of the more important characters as the series moves on. There would be no Series Two for Facinelli, however: his character gets run over and killed.

Away from the film set, he is happily married to Garth, and has three children – Luca Bella, Lola Ray and Fiona Eve. He is happily settled in his family life – seemingly speaking more about how happy he is as a dad than about the movies he is meant to be promoting.

While they spend time at their LA home, they also own a six-acre ranch outside the city – the latter being a haven for Garth. 'I'm really crazy about animals, and he doesn't really like them,' she said.

As you can imagine, with four special ladies in it, the Facinelli household is very female-dominated. 'You need a lot of patience,' he says.

Garth has commented in the media in the past, 'Sometimes I'll hear the Harley thing rev up, and I'll know he's had enough oestrogen for one day and he's gotta get out of the house. There's a lot of hormones going on right now in my house.'

Facinelli added, 'I grew up with three sisters. I was destined to be surrounded by women, I think. I'm used to it now and it's great.'

The couple have an incredibly loving relationship, but, as with many couples, there is the odd disagreement.

'Marriage requires work,' said Facinelli. 'It's when you push through those tough times that your relationship goes to the next level and you fall even deeper in love.'

They text each other constantly, and when they are apart filming they make sure they give each other gifts while they're holed up in a hotel.

'I'll send him his favourite tea to get him through the day. I make sure there is always something to keep him happy in his hotel room,' said Garth.

He is desperate to be a doting dad, and makes sure that he's there as often as he can be. Even now, he still coaches his daughters' soccer team (while filming *Hollow Man 2* he commuted from Vancouver to LA to catch their games) and ensures that their evening meal together is one filled with warmth and laughter. However, there is one rule that needs to be obeyed. He recalled, 'So now I started this new thing: I got this little wooden star, and I call it "the talking star". We all take turns holding the talking star so everybody's not talking at once. It's funny, if you talk out of order now my two-year-old gets mad, like, "You don't have the talking star!"'

A blue plate in the house was also a coveted item in the Facinelli–Garth household. If a member of the family has done something of note, they get to eat from the special plate – be it one of the girls who got a goal during a soccer match or Facinelli or Garth landing a part.

However, clumsy Garth smashed the blue plate in the kitchen. She recalled, 'Everyone screamed, "No!" We all freaked out. I was like, "What are we going to do?"'

Movie nights, bingo nights, watching Garth while she competed on US reality show *Dancing with the Stars* (their children weren't allowed to see his performance in the grown-up drama *Damages*) are all regular activities in their household.

Workwise, the offers were flooding in. But he was still looking for a part that he could sink his teeth into.

However, when he was first asked if he wanted to star in *Twilight* he wasn't keen at all. In a weird twist of fate, he was in an office when he noticed a book about vampires in movies. Although he wasn't a horror fan, he was drawn to the huge tome, and, as he began flicking through the pages and seeing their evolution in Hollywood, he realised just how beautiful and mysterious those films of old were.

Fearing that *Twilight* would be just another gore-and-guts vampire movie as seemed to be the modern trend, he passed on the chance to star in the film. It could have been a disastrous decision – one that he would have regretted for the rest of his life. Luckily, he was persuaded by his agent at least to read the source material.

'I read the book in a day and I fell in love with it. I thought it was a great story. It's like a throwback to the old Béla Lugosi movies, where it had the mystery and seductiveness of the old stories. That is why I enjoyed vampire movies. Somewhere along the line they became horror zombie movies and so that's what I thought when I first heard of it, but when I read it and realised that it wasn't about that, I said sign me up!'

However, after nearly passing on the chance, he was heartbroken to discover he'd failed the audition.

'I thought I did a great job and Catherine [Hardwicke, the director] liked me, but there was another actor that the studio was pushing for. I guess he was doing another movie or they couldn't work out his deal or something. But, when I read, I loved Catherine. She's full of passion and energy. I thought she was great and I really wanted to work with her. So, when I found out I didn't get the role, I was bummed.'

It's thought that the other actor was the British star Henry Cavill (Charles Brandon in *The Tudors*), and that he was *Twilight* author Stephenie Meyer's first choice to play Edward Cullen – but since he was 25, and with a potential four-film franchise, it was going to be hard to keep him looking like a 17-year-old.

During the early development, Meyer posted on her website, 'Indisputably the most difficult character to cast, Edward is also the one that I'm most passionately decided upon. The only actor I've ever seen who I think could come close to pulling off Edward Cullen is Henry Cavill. Henry was Albert, the young son in *The Count of Monte Cristo*. Can you see it? I know I can!'

Following *Twilight*'s success, Cavill told *MTV*, 'What I've heard, or pieced together from various sources, is that Stephenie had seen me in whatever jobs I had done previously, and I was probably perfect then! But, then, the ravages of time had taken their toll. By the time the movie came around, I didn't look right for the character.'

When it became obvious that Cavill was too old to play the part, Meyer wrote, 'The most disappointing thing for me is losing my perfect Edward. I'm not willing to relinquish Henry completely ... I propose that Henry play Carlisle!'

According to Henrycavillfan.com, the William

Morris Agency confirmed that he was offered the script but turned down the chance to audition for any role.

While Facinelli was clearly distraught, fate stepped in. He was in a bookshop when he happened to notice the vampire book he had flicked through while considering auditioning for *Twilight*. Thinking nothing of it, he sent the book to Hardwicke, with a note saying, 'Look, I'm sorry it didn't work out. I really admire your work. I hope this book inspires you through the making of *Twilight*.'

As luck would have it, Hardwicke received the go-ahead to cast Carlisle Cullen again. And, just as she was beginning to come up with a list of new names, she spied the book on her desk and thought of Facinelli.

He said, 'So I always joke that I bought the role of Dr Carlisle Cullen for $29.99. And I was worth every penny.'

The challenge of bringing Carlisle to life was obvious to Facinelli. He was hundreds of years old, and his performance had to reflect that. He studied old paintings, read books, gave himself 'a silly gait to the way he walked' and added a suggestion of British to his accent – the reasoning being that he would have had a British accent, but it would have become diluted during his long stay in the USA.

'Whenever you take on a role there are things you connect with and things you have to research, and for me, being a patriarch of a family came naturally,' he said. 'I have a family of my own and so I understood what it was like. So it was more about working on who Carlisle was as a person and where his travels have taken him and how to get 350 years onto the screen.'

chapter four

The Mother

'You have to have more than a dream. It's hard, and getting harder every day. You have to really want it and be determined to do just about anything to get it.' – Elizabeth Reaser

Anyone who knew Elizabeth Reaser while she was growing up in Michigan would have guessed she was destined to be a performer. She grew up 'subjecting my family to really bad shows in the living room'.

'It's what I love to do,' she added.

She was born on 15 June 1975 in Michigan to Karen Davidson and John Reaser, an attorney cum restaurateur cum substitute teacher. Her parents divorced when she was young and her mother married billionaire businessman William Davidson. In 2009, her stepdad died aged 86, and Karen became the owner of the basketball team Detroit Pistons.

She is the middle of three sisters and has said in interviews that she's the hardest-working of all of them, and the least spoilt. 'The ones before and after me were. I'm still waiting,' she joked in an interview.

She first went to an all-girls Catholic elementary school, which Reaser described as 'very hardcore.' When she attended her high school, she was delighted that it was a mixed school because she 'was really into boys and just liked to party'. The new environment was 'totally new and crazy' for the young Reaser, who also worked a number of odd jobs, including that of a caddy at a country club. 'But the tips were good and, hanging around the caddy shack, I met lots of boys,' she added.

Boys were certainly on her mind when she was a teenager. If her parents were worried that her daughter was focusing more on them than on her education, then she gave them the scare of their lives when she was 16.

'I ran away in the middle of the night, got on a train and went to California. I had a boyfriend who had moved out there, and I thought California sounded so cool. It always just captured my imagination. I remember drinking and smoking cigarettes out the window and just being a total rock star in my own mind.'

Her parents, being understandably worried, eventually 'figured out where I was and basically said, "You're either going to come home, or you're going to be arrested and incarcerated."'

She added, 'So I came home. It was really dramatic, though, at the time.'

She was accepted into Oakland University, but after a short time there she became desperate for change. 'It was really a fine school, but I yearned to get out of the Midwest and I realised the only way my parents were going to let me was through college, so I applied to Juilliard's drama programme,' she said, referring to the Juilliard School at the Lincoln Center for the Performing Arts in New York City.

She had impressed at high school with her acting prowess, especially when playing Helena in a production of *A Midsummer Night's Dream*.

Seeking her parents' approval, which they duly gave, much to her shock, she studied drama at the prestigious acting school after impressing them with a Shakespeare monologue for her audition.

However, she found that 'every day was a struggle' at the school. 'But I'm so glad now I did it because it gave me all this technical skill I never thought I'd need.' While it was certainly an intense and stressful period, it was one she persevered with, receiving a bachelor's degree in fine arts in 1999.

Although Juilliard 'opened a few doors', Reaser would still have to find acting roles where she 'could invite agents and hope against hope that they'd come and see me'. She moaned, 'It was difficult and frustrating. You couldn't get good jobs without an agent and you couldn't get an agent without having been seen in good roles. It's very competitive and agents are inundated with hundreds of requests for representation.'

She attended up to 14 auditions a week in a bid to achieve her dream. 'Like so many actors I had to sometimes work part-time to make ends meet, especially when I told my family that I wanted to be on my own. For a while, I was a waitress and it just wasn't fun.

'You have to have more than a dream. It's hard, and getting harder every day. You have to really want it and be determined to do just about anything to get it. And you have to stay very focused. I feel so blessed that I've been able to achieve what I have without a lot of pain and struggle. There are so many actors out there who are immensely talented and some I know are pretty close to starving. Even in what I would call my lean times, I never approached that; but, thankfully, I also had a lot of support from my family.'

Reaser would impress with a breakout role in the daytime US drama *Guiding Light*. She then found herself excelling in a number of stage productions, including a revival of Tennessee's Williams's *Sweet Bird of Youth* and Shakespeare's *The Winter's Tale* alongside David Strathairn and Barbara Garrick.

As someone who was desperate to tread the boards, she was delighted when she went on to star in London's West End in a critically acclaimed production of the intense play *Blackbird* by Adam Rapp. 'It was an exciting, intense experience,' she said of her time in the production, which saw her play a Lower East Side addict who stays with her abusive boyfriend because she has no other options.

Her delight at having to appear in the West End was nearly brought to an abrupt end over union problems. She explained to *Lifestyle* magazine, 'Just when we thought everything was set there were problems with getting the British acting union to have two Americans in roles that the union felt should be played by English actors. But somehow everything got resolved.

'The play was raw and intense, but the audience response was exhilarating. That made it all worthwhile. The thing that struck me the most was number of young people in the audience. We were in a small theater where the tickets weren't priced out of the stratosphere, so that was a plus.'

Although for the first time in her life she was getting fan mail from her success in the play, she also remembered on one occasion performing to only two audience members! Still, she made sure she gave it her all. 'I'd like to think that I worked just as hard in that play, even though there were more people on stage than in the audience.'

While as a child she dreamed of appearing on stage, she was beginning to yearn for a new acting challenge. 'I really wanted to do plays, since I was a little girl. I wanted to go to Juilliard and to learn, but then I really fell in love with doing film and television along the way.'

She was to bag roles in *The Believer*, *Thirteen Conversations About One Thing* and the 2002 thriller *Emmett's Mark*.

Honoured by *Interview* magazine as one of the '14 To Be: Emerging Creative Women', she would go on to star in a number of TV movies, pilots and feature films, including working once more with her *Believer* co-star Ryan Gosling in *Stay*. The psychological thriller also featured Ewan McGregor, Bob Hoskins and Naomi Watts.

Next up was the sweet and charming drama *Sweet Land*, based on the 1989 short story 'A Gravestone Made of Wheat' by Will Weaver. The author explained the plot as being 'about the promise of love, it's about a mail-order bride who arrives on a promise and full of faith – but upon her arrivals she is unable to get citizen papers and cannot get married.'

Talking about Reaser's casting, director Ali Selim revealed, 'Fearing [her character Inge's] German accent and her lack of celebrity, she tried to get her agent to cancel. Gratefully, her agent would not. She came into an open casting and stumbled through the Norwegian with the German accent and I was charmed and committed. I usually make a strong effort to say to actors in an audition, "Thanks for coming in" rather than "Nice to meet you" and definitely not "See you soon" – the ultimate sign of hope. To Elizabeth I foolishly, winsomely said, "You're beautiful."'

Speaking about working with the likes of Ned Beatty and Allan Cumming in the movie, Reaser noted, 'At first it was intimidating, but then, after you meet them and see how they work, not at all. I learned so much just from observing Mr Beatty, who was extremely supportive. And Alan is hilarious and a really nice guy.'

It was well received by the critics, with *Variety* saying, 'This intelligently written, brilliantly cast and thesped story of a German mail-order bride in a Norwegian-American community in Minnesota just after WWI never hits a wrong note.'

Reaser was singled out for praise: 'Reaser's Inge is a marvel of strength, humor and sensuality, any hint of anachronism deftly sidestepped by the fact that her emotional outbursts of enthusiasm or anger are delivered in an expressive but un-subtitled mix of German and Norwegian.'

Sweet Land won her the Jury Award at the Newport Beach Film Festival and an independent Spirit Award.

The 2005 'dramedy' *The Family Stone* saw Reaser play one of the many family members of Diane Keaton and Craig T. Nelson's characters. It tells the story of a man (Dermot Mulroney) bringing home his uptight girlfriend (Sarah Jessica Parker) to his dysfunctional family.

'Craig T. Nelson has long been one of my favourite actors,' revealed Reaser. 'So having the opportunity to work with him was such a pleasure. Diane Keaton is not only an incredible actress and an incredibly nice person, but she's the coolest lady. It's great when you're working and having such a marvellous, memorable time.'

Reaser again impressed in *Puccini for Beginners*, in

which she played a bisexual woman. Reaser explained why she thought she was considered for the part. 'I think she [director Maria Maggenti] considered me bisexual. I read with Gretchen Mol, and we had, like, chemistry. I probably could be bisexual.'

It was a part that Reaser loved playing, 'The script was so sexy and different and smart, I just wanted to be Allegra so badly it was killing me. When I got it, I was screaming and calling everyone, like I usually do.'

Her next role would be something of an irony for Reaser – she would star in the short-lived US medical drama *Saved*. 'I'm potentially a really bad hypochondriac, so I have to be careful. I mean, it's pretty mild. I'm not like a real hypochondriac. But, if I thought about something for long enough or if I went on the Internet and read too much about certain symptoms, I could probably start to create some serious issues for myself.'

However, she was desperate to take the role seriously, and made sure she did the required research. She attended emergency rooms (ERs) and hung out with a medical staff in a bid to insert some realism into the part.

'Humour is the only way to make it through these intense, frightening situations that our characters face. I hung out in an ER when I was researching for this role and I found that the doctors were really funny. They were always finding the humour within these frightening situations. Humour is real. Within any drama in anyone's life, there's always a way to find humour in it. Without humour no one cares about whatever drama is going on.'

When *Saved* ended, she found herself appearing in another hospital drama – this time *Grey's Anatomy*, playing a disfigured Jane Doe. 'Her face has been smashed – like every bone in her face – and there are issues with her chest. There's a lot of work to be done to put her back together,' she said of her character.

To achieve that look, she had to undergo three-hour daily makeup sessions. She had to suffer several discomforts, including the prosthetics that remained on her face for the 12-hour shoot and a daily food diet that included only smoothies or small helpings of soft foods.

Her *Puccini for Beginners* co-star Justin Kirk called her 'Elephant Reaser' – while her *Saved* colleague Michael McMillan said she'd be perfect for the lead role in *Mask 2*!

'Some of the jokes are funny, and some of them are not,' she said.

Reaser was meant to appear in only a few episodes, but her performance earned her a prolonged stay of 17. She was nominated for a Primetime Emmy Award for her role.

Her roles in the hospital dramas were tinged with more irony, as the actress suffered a terrifying near-death experience. She had been travelling to Las Vegas with a female friend when her Jeep Cherokee flew off the freeway at a speed of up to 65mph, flipping twice in the air and going down into a ravine.

She said, 'It was the most insane, horrifying thing. We were in shock, so we couldn't move. We were lying in the desert, strapped down [by paramedics], waiting to be taken to the hospital.'

Despite the fact that Reaser's car was written off, she and her friend both, amazingly, escaped unhurt. She recalled, 'We were a little sore, but not a scratch. When I got this part, it reminded me of the shock and fear that I experienced that day. You just feel so vulnerable.'

Her success on *Grey's Anatomy* led to her being cast in *The Ex List*, a comedy TV series about a woman's search for love, which was based on the Israeli series *The Mythological X*. She filmed the pilot for *The Ex List*, while also filming an intense episode of *Grey's Anatomy* – and it was definitely hard for Reaser to balance the two tonally different shows.

'I did the pilot and literally we wrapped on Saturday night at five in the morning for the pilot and I had Sunday to take all my stuff back to LA from San Diego. And Monday morning I started shooting the episode where I was having the hysterical pregnancy on *Grey's Anatomy* and having the nervous breakdown. It was such a trip and weird and wild.'

Describing *The Ex List*, she said, 'It's a romantic comedy. The whole premise is that my character Bella Bloom goes to a psychic randomly at a bachelorette party and the psychic says, "You've already met and dated the love of your life and you're supposed to marry him. And if you don't find him within a year you're going to spend the rest of your life alone." And so begins this quest to find love. The motivation is really pure for Bella. It's not about finding a man. It's not about some desperate idea of marriage. It's about love and connection. And it's hilarious. Because you do really ridiculous things when you're trying to fall in love.'

Explaining why she loved the part, she said, 'I did a film called *Puccini for Beginners*, which was a romantic comedy, and I always wanted to do more, but I kept doing drama. It's an easy thing for me tap into. This is more challenging: to work at a different speed, quicker and lighter. It seems easy and fun, but it's more subtle and it's actually harder.'

However, she insisted she is not in a rush to the altar like her character. 'My older sister is married and that took a lot of pressure off me. She had the greatest wedding of all time, the three most beautiful children of all time, and her husband is the greatest brother-in-law you could ever ask for. So I'm covered; I can go be a crazy-actress diva.'

She added in another interview, '[My parents] want me married and they want grandkids. Thanks to my older sister, they have that. She's delivered. For a while there, they were waiting for me to deliver, but they realise they have an actress in the family. It's the oddest thing. Most parents wouldn't want that, but mine seem so happy for me. I'm not saying that they don't worry about my financial future, but they've seen how exciting it's been.'

While Reaser impressed, the show was hit by a series of backstage problems. Its creator Diane Ruggiero quit, over what the CBS called, 'a simple disagreement about the future direction of the show, particularly as it pertains to Bella'.

The disagreement stemmed from the tone of the series. CBS's president of entertainment, Nina Tassler, said, 'In the Israeli series, the character had a sense of adventure and wonderment and optimism. We just wanted to make sure that in the scenes and in the stories we were faithful to that.'

Reaser said at the time, 'Unfortunately, they don't tell actors anything. All I know is that Diane resigned and I adore her and absolutely respect her decision completely. And at the same time I'm really excited about doing the show. I definitely feel like we have awesome writers and amazing producers. Honestly, I don't know enough about it to make a comment.'

Sadly for Reaser, the show would end after just one series.

She wasn't to know it, but she was to about to star in one of the biggest Hollywood crazes in years.

When she attended the audition for Esme Cullen in *Twilight*, she had no idea that the job she was auditioning for was going to be such a big deal. 'I had never heard of the books before the audition. In fact,

Catherine Hardwicke told me in the audition that it was a book because I was like, "What the hell is going on here?"'

To get into character, Reaser devoured all the books and fan blogs on the website.

She told *Vanity Fair*, 'When you have the material there's so much already on the page from Stephenie's [Meyer's] imagination. Most of it came from that; she's got so much backstory. There's so much on the Internet, actually, which I found really interesting because they write about your character, they write about all of our characters. I found it really fascinating – their take on it. Even on YouTube, they'll have some kind of report on Esme or Carlisle and their relationship and it's just been really interesting.'

The feisty and headstrong Reaser, who at one point looked as if she was aiming to be the queen of independent cinema, was about to be one of the most famous mothers on the big screen.

chapter five
The Beefcake

'I feel for the people who just want to be famous, because your eyes are going to be opened. It's not pretty when you're working, and then you've got six months where you aren't.' – Kellan Lutz

Kellan Lutz didn't know why, but he was obsessed with signing his autograph as a youngster. He remembers 'just having fun doing it for no reason'. He added, 'I'd always want to sign a cheque when I was younger so I was, like, practising.' Good thing, too, because the young hunk actor certainly has had to sign a lot of autographs recently.

He was born in North Dakota on 15 March 1985 to a fairly large household – he has six brothers and one sister. However, despite all his many siblings, he still managed to stand out – and was in fact nicknamed Krazy Kellan by his family members.

Moving 'around the Midwest and landing in Arizona', where his mother remarried, Lutz worked incredibly hard at high school in a bid to make sure he could attend a university of some standing.

'I had so many siblings that it was a financial issue, as far as going to a better school, because of all the boys. So, however hard you worked in school and the scholarships you got, that's where you could go. We had limitations, so I worked my butt off to get to any school in California just because my father had been living there since I was six.

'That's when the divorce happened. And I really wanted to get close to him because I never really had much of a relationship with him. I'd see him once or twice a year. So our plan worked and I ended up getting a lot of scholarships for a lot of schools there, and I chose Orange County's Chapman University to attend, just because it was the OC and it was closer to my father. And the school was great and they gave me the most money. I was going there for chemical engineering. It was kind of crazy, but I love chemistry and engineering. It was one of those things that my mother just pushed me toward the most.'

Lutz earned some money in LA, modelling. He had done some modelling work in Arizona, but he found that LA was a lot different in that aspect. 'I've been modelling since I was thirteen or fourteen, right when I hit Arizona. I was trying to make extra money. Once I got to LA, the modelling market was a lot bigger, so I was, like, "Wow, you can make this much money? That's ten times as much money as in Arizona!"'

While he would eventually work for Abercrombie & Fitch, and has recently been the face of Calvin Klein, it's not something he ever considered as his ultimate career move. But, while he was sure modelling wasn't where he saw his future, neither was chemical engineering.

He had done a 'little theatre stuff for my church, growing up, like every year doing the Christmas play and *Oliver Twist*, and fun stuff like that' – but he thought it was just something to pass the time and not take seriously as a career move. However, being surrounded by so many wannabe actors in LA piqued his interest and Lutz began taking classes.

When he quickly landed a manager and then his first call-back he assumed he was on his way to Hollywood success. With the end of the first semester at Chapman looming, it was to be a costly error.

Talking to Mediablvd.com, he recalled, 'I had to decide what to do. I thought call-backs meant that it would be down to me and one other guy, and I would get the role. I couldn't do finals because I thought that would start my career. And, wow, was I wrong! I did the call-back and didn't go further at all. I realised there were three other call-backs after that, and then a screen test, and then you get it. I was really bummed, and I failed all those classes. The hardest decision in my life was to tell my mother.

'And she had no idea what acting really was. Coming from the Midwest, acting was unheard of.

We had four or five channels back then, and you never really thought that real people were on these shows. I never even knew acting was a profession and an occupation.'

So, Lutz put school on hold, saying 'you can always go back to school. I was 18, at the time, and I just wanted to do it. I didn't really have too much support from my mother, with that decision. I was on my own.

'But, thank God my father was there. I just hung out with him when I was lonely or just wanted to hang out because I didn't really know anyone in California. I really just put all of me into what I was going to do, and got myself an agent and went to as many classes as I could. I learned as much as I could, as fast as I could. I have a great team now. They've been pushing me and the ball's been rolling great. I have no regrets. I love the decision I made, and I always will.'

Because Lutz was brought up loving sport and other activities, he approached acting as something of a hobby rather than as a destined calling like other wannabe actors. He didn't take it as seriously as others, and be believes that is something that has made him stand out.

'I'm not going to cry if I don't work. I have the most fun just being normal and doing regular stuff.

'That differs from people who move out from somewhere like Florida, who have to make it their first year or it's the end of the world, and they become depressed and move back home because they're a failure. You can't just become a movie star. I feel for the people who just want to be famous, because your eyes are going to be opened. It's not pretty when you're working, and then you've got six months where you aren't. You feel like a failure. It's tough, and a lot of people lose sight of who they really are. I have great parents. As hard as it was, my mother was a great mother. She put great feet on me and a good head on my shoulders.'

And his approach to acting seemed to pay dividends: he bagged a 2004 role in the *Bold and Beautiful*. It may have been a minor role but it was enough to get him further work in the reality show *Model Citizens*, *CSI: NY*, *Six Feet Under*, *Summerland* and *The Comeback*.

He was to make his big screen debut in 2006 in the athletics movie *Stick It*, which also featured Jeff Bridges. Critics were less than impressed with the drama – with *Sight and Sound* calling it 'a leaden-footed hybrid of sports movie and teen comedy', and *Empire* saying it 'was far from a perfect ten'.

But it was a role that proved to be a great vindication for Lutz who had taken a huge risk in turning his back on his university studies. 'And now my mother is happy because I brought her to the *Stick It* premiere for Disney. It was a gymnastics movie. She looked so beautiful, and just had so much fun seeing what Hollywood and acting really is, and that it's not the negative occupation that she thought it was. Everything is great now.'

Next up was for Lutz was a role in the Justin Long comedy *Accepted*. Two thousand and six also saw him appear in an advert for the fragrance called With Love … Hilary Duff, and he also appeared in the singer's video for her pop song 'With Love'.

He would return to the small screen with appearances in *CSI* and *Heroes*, and land a part in HBO's *Generation Kill*. Based on the book by Evan Wright, it was adapted for the screen by *The Wire*'s David Simon and Ed Burns in 2008.

He was so desperate to star in the show saying that his 'team called ahead of time and said, "Kellan is really interested in this, so just make sure you watch the tape," because they were getting thousands of tapes. I auditioned for it, and the casting director just really had a great eye, as far as what was going to be needed.

'I believe the casting director really thought about, "Is this guy going to be easy to work with? He's a great actor, but is he going to be a pain for seven months, or is he going to be able to do it?" Let's be honest, anyone could play Jason Lilley, and anyone could play some of the other guys. Yes, I made choices that I think helped me to get it, but I'm not saying that I'm the only one who could play him. There are a lot of surfer-type, blond-haired, blue-eyed guys out there. But it was great. We made it easy. There were no fights at all. It was just guys being guys, and we had so much fun.'

While other actors struggled with the boot camp – which was vital to show the actors the physical rigors that soldiers go through – the hugely confident and athletic Lutz, unsurprisingly, loved every moment of it. 'It was meant to be a three-week boot camp but got reduced because the other actors couldn't do it.'

While they filmed in Mozambique, the actors would 'get together at six in the morning and go for a run'.

He added, 'I really found a passion for running, which was really cool. The training was really, really intense. People threw up, every day. The best part about it was that we'd have classroom training also, just like at real boot camp, and they would talk to us about all the weaponry and what the rounds would do and how far they would go. Just seeing all of us actors, wearing all of our Marine get-up in the classroom, we were Marines, at that point. It was real. It was really cool.'

Filming the show in Mozambique was something of a culture shock for Lutz. Every day he and the rest of the cast and crew made sure they were carrying a wad of cash on them. Just walking to the nearest market would result in their being stopped by soldiers looking for a bribe. According to Lutz, 'In Mozambique, they'd just had their civil war about ten years ago and we're walking down the street and there are guys strapped with AK-47s.

'If we left the hotel we'd get arrested. They'd call you over… and you don't wanna run, 'cause they'll shoot you. They'll be like, "You're coming to jail," and you'd be like, "How much money can I give you to not go to jail?" We hid money everywhere because if you go the market you get stopped three times and, if you don't have money, you're screwed. I can't believe we all made it back safely.'

Instead they stayed in their hotels and partied a lot!

At the premiere, he noted, 'She [his mother] came out to my *Generation Kill* premiere with my stepfather, who was actually in the Air Force, and it was fun, bringing them out here. They drove out, and I took them to dinner and paid for it. I wanted to do that because they've done so much for me and now it's all about giving back. I had a lot of help, throughout the years. I remember telling my mom, when I was in middle school, "One day I'm going to build your dream house. Whatever you want, I'm going to build it." It was such a dream, but it's actually going to come true, one day. It's going to be fun to actually do that.'

Films like *Deep Winter* and *Prom Night* were next – with the latter, a horror remake, sliced apart by critics. *Empire* wrote, 'By the time the killer in this lame slasher movie starts hacking up the gormless cast, you'll be pleased to hear the last of their inane chatter.'

He would then land a part as George Evans in *90210* – a remake of the nineties TV hit *Beverly Hills 90210* – of which he remarked, 'I love that show. It's going amazing. The cast is so cool. I'm working with a lot of friends, which always makes it easy. My character, George Evans, is the cocky dick of the school who just doesn't care. He's from a rich family. If he got suspended, he'd pay his way out. He's supposed to be the lacrosse star, and then Dixon [Tristan Wilds] comes in and steals his thunder, so he really gets pissed [off]. He never likes to be second place. I'm having a lot of fun playing him.'

While he would go on to play the character in only six episodes because of the success of a certain vampire series, he would embark on a reported on/off romance with his co-star on the show – AnnaLynne McCord. Not that Lutz would ever kiss and tell when it came to divulging any details.

When asked about his romance with McCord, he told Ryan Seacrest on his KISS-FM radio, 'Oh. No. Never have been. I've known her for six years, and we met again on the set of *90210* but we shot Abercrombie [catalogues] way back in the day. She's single, and I'm very much single.'

In a weird way, Kellan was always destined to play a vampire. He told his agent at the start of 2007 that he should be told of any scripts coming up that featured marines, vampires or boxers. When casting for *Twilight* began, Lutz was still in Africa filming *Generation Kill*.

'At the time, my agent was sending me out for Edward, the main character. I read it and it was just too hard to put myself on tape because I was in a Third World country and, if you send a DVD, there's probably one-tenth of a chance that it will get to America. I don't care to be the lead of everything. I just like playing characters that really grab me. So, when I saw the character of Emmett, I thought he would just be such a cool character to play. I was like, "Hey, I want this Emmett guy. He's cool."'

But the project was already cast, meaning it looked as if Lutz had missed out on his dream role. Dejected, he decided to take a break from acting after his work on *Generation Kill* ended. He wanted to take a short time off to focus on spending some time with his family and friends.

However, he was to get a second bite at starring in *Twilight*. Lutz told an interviewer, 'The actor who was playing Emmett fell through, for whatever reason. So I said, "Get me in there!" The next day, my agent said, "Your audition is tomorrow. If they like you, they're going to fly you to Oregon the next day." I went to the audition and there were five of my other friends there and, in the end, they liked me and this other guy. Then it came down to them liking me, just a little bit more. I really think Ashley Greene put in a good word and said, "Kellan's awesome to work with!"

'I had a lot of people rooting for me. So they flew me out to Oregon that night, and I had to audition for Catherine Hardwicke the next morning, at eight o'clock. It just happened so fast, and I only packed one outfit. So I did the audition at eight o'clock, and Catherine liked me a lot and said, "You're my perfect Emmett! You're it!" And, I was so excited because I was playing a vampire. I loved the script and I loved

Emmett. Then, they sent me home a couple days later and I packed up. I was just so excited.

'And, I really didn't realise what *Twilight* was. I honestly didn't realise the huge cult following, and that there were so many books. I was just excited that someone wrote an amazing script that was so sensual. It's beautiful. It's a love story about a vampire and a human girl, and what they can and cannot do. It was just really cool. So, once I found out that there were books, I did myself some reading and fell in love with the whole series.'

He had played a marine, and he was set to play a vampire. While he was still on the lookout to play a boxer, he certainly had to fight to get a role in *Twilight*. But his audition was a knockout, and he was now set to star in a heavyweight of a blockbuster.

chapter six
The Indie Queen

'I thought the film would solve all her problems.' – Catherine Hardwicke

Born on 17 May 1988 to a family comprising of a beautician mother, a set designer dad and an older brother, Nikki Reed spent what can probably best be described as an eventful childhood.

When she was two, her parents divorced. She lived with her mother, Cheryl, in their LA home, where she spent a lot of her time reading books. She was a shy child, whose love of horseback riding would see her head to the stables every week. 'My grandma breeds them,' she said.

However, when she was about to become a teenager, she became obsessed with her appearance. Her best friend would come over at half past four in the morning so they could spend nearly three hours putting on their makeup and doing their hair before they went to school, with their evenings spent deciding on what to wear.

She has said in the past, 'I had a calendar with a list of my wardrobe, down to how I wore my hair, so I wouldn't ever wear the same outfit again.'

A backpack was deemed too unfashionable to wear, so she would carry a handbag, into which she just about managed to fit a couple of pens and pieces of paper. Not that Reed seemed to care: she was too worried about attending gym classes because she thought her legs were too fat.

Of course, low-self-esteem issues are nothing new with youngsters – and certainly the stunning actress should have had no such worries. However, it was a way of life for the young Reed, as it is for many girls. What makes Reed extraordinary, though, is that she managed to turn her childhood into an explosive and controversial movie.

It all happened when her dad's ex-girlfriend noticed that something was wrong with the young girl. At this point, Reed was 'hanging out with the bad girls, ditching school, smoking weed and messing around with boys'.

Reed's father's ex-girlfriend – a certain Catherine Hardwicke – has known Nikki Reed since she was five and she was struck by how much she had changed. Hardwicke took the teenager for a walk on the beach for a chat. Their outings were to be a regular occurrence, and they would go to museums, surf together or head to photo exhibitions in a bid to 'open her mind up', remarked Hardwicke. They would talk and talk – with Reed opening up more and more to Hardwicke with every meeting.

Reed recalled, 'I guess Catherine's intentions were a little bit different than mine… I had no idea that was what was going on in her brain. I just sat down with her and thought we were having fun together.'

Hardwicke wasn't a director at this point – but she was in the movie business working as a production designer. And it was she who suggested to Reed that they work together on a screenplay.

During a school holiday, Hardwicke and Reed would spend six days writing the script. What Hardwicke found interesting was Reed's relationship with her mother. Talking about her mother, Reed recalled, 'She's a very, very sweet woman, and it's really hard for her to see my brother and I upset. And so it's just, like, "OK, whatever you want." But, at a certain point, we started to take advantage of that and we started walking all over her. But there was a lot of love in the house.'

Reed struggled at first, coming to terms with the script. She recalled, 'There were points where it was really frustrating, when Catherine was like, "Nikki, here's this notepad. I need you to go and write down every funny thing your mom says." I'm like, "What? My mom's not funny. What would I do?" I think there were times like that when it was really frustrating, and

Catherine would say, "You're not looking at this from my point of view. Your mom is a great woman and there's many other points to her." It happened so fast, though, that it wasn't like a three-year process where there weren't that many rewrites.

'I knew nothing about writing. But Catherine wasn't thirteen and I was, so that's where the movie got its basic outline. It's my voice. The number-one rule of writing is write what you know – or something like that,' added Reed. 'So I wrote about my experiences.'

These experiences seemed to shock America when the film, *Thirteen*, was released in 2003, with some viewers stunned at the film's depiction of underage sex, self-harm and drink and drug abuse.

The film was a huge critical hit nonetheless – with Holly Hunter and Evan Rachel Wood, who played mother and daughter in the movie, receiving nominations for Golden Globes. Hunter was also nominated for an Academy award.

Wood's character Tracy was loosely based on Reed and, because of this, she expected to play the role. But she would play Tracy's friend, Evie, instead.

Delighted by reaction to the film, Hardwicke believed at the time, 'the film would solve all her problems.'

Unfortunately, it didn't work out that way. Reed made her way back to high school, expecting to make a 'ton of new friends'. 'It was really horrible writing a film about not being able to fit in and hoping this would help and then going back and having the problem start all over again.'

She was still an outsider – albeit one who was now something of a movie star. Growing tired of 'mothers who were sneaking into the school at lunchtime to confront and harass her about the film' she went into home schooling. She was living by herself at this point, so, as you can imagine, 'it didn't really work out because you tell a kid who lives by themselves to go to school and teach themselves... yeah, right. So I graduated and I took my GED [general education diploma] and then I actually went back to school and got my high school diploma.'

Reuniting with Hardwicke on skater drama *Lords of Dogtown* reaffirmed Reed's indie credentials – as did *Mini's First Time*, a drama that tells the story of a character played by Nikki Reed embarking on an affair with her stepfather, played by Alec Baldwin.

Reed continued with her writing, and she had her heart set on filming a script set in New Zealand, which she wrote. However, she was advised to take a role on popular US teen series *The O.C.* (standing for Orange County), in which she played Sadie Campbell for a handful of episodes.

Reed explained, 'I had a discussion with my team about it. They came to me and said, "You know, Nikki, if you really want your script to get made, if you really want someone to give you money for this, and unfortunately, you have to compromise. You have to do something." To be on the show that undeniably seven million viewers a night watch... to be recognised and appreciated by a younger audience makes you more marketable.

'If it doesn't have the same level of integrity, it has something that *Thirteen* didn't have, which is a much bigger audience and money.'

However, she was becoming frustrated with the system – which was somewhat ironic, as she was only now really starting to fall in love with acting.

When she was 16, she 'moved out and couldn't go back to school and that was my only choice. And so I acted to pay the bills. Now I'm acting because I enjoy it. And that's all I can say about it, because it's not going to be the rest of my life.'

She knew she had versatile talents, but her previous sex-bomb roles were leaving her typecast.

'I haven't really been given the opportunity to stretch in other stuff, and that's unfortunate. I get some scripts and my agent says, "You should read this if you like it, but you can't go in and even meet on it because they don't want to meet you." And I think that's so ignorant. I don't want to use the word "naïve" because I don't think that it's strong enough.

'I'm very fortunate and very happy to be where I'm at, and very proud of the choices that I've made, but it's hurt my feelings – to walk into a room of producers and say here's why I love this role and here's why I can play this and have them say, "No, but it was nice meeting you; we'll call you when we have [a part for] Angelina Jolie's little sister" – I don't think that's very fair.'

However, her mentor was to step in with a script that Reed immediately fell for.

Hardwicke said, 'When I read *Twilight*, I thought Nikki would be perfect for Rosalie. When I called her to talk about the part, she said, "Everyone will want Bella and Edward to be together. Rosalie is trying to break them up – so they hate me. I'm OK with that."'

Reed faced a severe backlash from the online community following her casting as Rosalie Hale – the long-term girlfriend of Emmett Cullen. And it was clear that the criticism hurt her, with her pleading, 'What I want to say to the fans is, "You have no idea how badly I want to make this right for you."'

However, she knew that she would be vindicated when fans saw the film – and she fell back on advice her father had given her. After she'd broken up with her boyfriend, she became worried about what their shared friends would think, and was desperate to give them her side of the story. However, her dad said, 'You have to be patient. And remember that people are smarter than you think they are and you don't have to convince them of anything and eventually they will figure it out.'

And it was advice she used following the backlash from the online forums. 'I remember what my father said and I realise that people will grow and they will mature. And that the people who are really negative in their own right, you can't change them. It's also really amazing that there's that much positivity. That is so genuine. Like when you meet people at malls and you do autograph signings. It's real. They slept on the floor for five days to see us, even if it's undeserved on our part. You have to take some of that in. And recognise that you are part of something that is so amazing and that has made such a connection.'

chapter seven

The Rock Star

'My friends and I were kind of the bad kids in school, the troublemakers.'
– Jackson Rathbone

Monroe Jackson Rathbone V was born in Singapore on 21 December 1984. While he would go on to live in America, he would find himself travelling all over the world, including places such as Indonesia, London and Norway, thanks to his father's job at Mobil Oil. (His great-grandfather, Monroe Jackson Rathbone II was the chairman of Standard Oil of New Jersey, which later became Exxon.) They eventually settled in Midland, Texas, where Rathbone found a huge love of theatre.

He joined the theatre group the Pickwick Players, which was primarily musical-based. As well as acting, Rathbone would also spend his time playing basketball, track, soccer, baseball and football – as well as temporarily starting up a mobile-DJ business!

Much to the delight of his dad, he would also play the role of protective brother to his three young sisters.

'When it comes to my sisters' boyfriends, I'm either cool with them or my sisters know that I hate them. I'm pretty blunt with them and to the point. Back in high school, there were a couple of boys my sisters had and, man, I let them know I didn't like them. I was pretty upfront but my dad always had it right. Whenever my sisters brought them over to the house for the first time, he'd be teaching me how to clean the shotguns.'

Much to his parents' displeasure, however, he moved to Michigan to attend the prestigious Interlochen Arts Academy – a private arts school where he majored in acting. His mother, Randee, remembered, 'We were not thrilled with the idea: we wanted him to stay and graduate from high school in Midland.'

He originally worked behind the stage at high school, working on set and lighting design, before he decided to go out front instead. 'When I started being onstage, I fell in love with it,' he admitted. He found that he loved classical plays, and was particularly impressive in Shakespeare productions.

While he thrived in that environment, he would also show his rebellious side at the Academy. He told *Inked* magazine, 'My friends and I were kind of the bad kids in school, the troublemakers. [We went to] this really great boarding school in Michigan, and there were six of us who were always acting out against authority. The school administration was like, "Stay away from those boys – they're Lost Boys" so that's what everyone called us.'

In fact, the 18-year-old Rathbone went on to get a tattoo that read 'I'M LOST'. He has previously talked about getting another tattoo.

He explained, 'I'd love to get the Rathbone family crest on my back – it would take up my whole back. Our motto is "*Suaviter et Fortiter*", which means "Nicely, but firmly". My dad always taught me that you've got to give respect to get respect, and you've got to give love to get love. Makes sense, right?'

The Lost Boys were the ones you went to if you wanted to get alcohol at the boarding school, with Rathbone revealing, 'Let's just say we had a lot of alcohol on the premises that we weren't supposed to have. We kept whiskey in shampoo bottles and vodka in conditioner bottles. A few of my friends were actually expelled.'

After graduating, he was stuck between going to the Royal Scottish Academy of Music and Drama and moving to LA in a bid to land acting work. One of his friends at Interlochen, Alex Boyd, was already in LA, and introduced Jackson to his manager, who promptly signed the young actor.

He quickly managed to land a job for Disney 411 – interviewing celebrities. He found work on shows such as *The O.C.* and *Close To Home* – with movie roles on films such as *Molding Clay*, *Pray for Morning* and *Travis and Henry*.

They were minor parts, but vital ones for his screen education. However, when he did land some bigger screentime roles – such as the one in the US series *Beautiful People* – he struggled. He said, 'It was my very first leading-man role. I'd only ever been a character actor in theatre, and I had never played the romantic leading man. I never really wanted to. I have a lot more fun playing characters.'

While acting is a huge passion for Rathbone, so is music. He is in a band called 100 Monkeys, with Ben Graupner and Ben Johnson, who were friends at school.

Rathbone explained, 'Once we all graduated, we all went to different areas. Ben Johnson went to New York and Ben Graupner went to Scotland. They both went to college, and I moved out to LA to do the acting thing. And then, finally, about a year ago, Ben Graupner moved out here to LA, and then Ben Johnson came out. We started playing together, and it just sounded so sweet. It was just so much fun.

'The idea of 100 Monkeys was something that we came up with. It's all improvisational music. It's like a jam band, except we do sing and make up lyrics. Whenever we record, the rule is that we only get one try. You can't have a redo. You can lay one thing down and do one set of over-dubs, but that's it. We try to break it down to a simple, natural, live, creative art type of thing, which is what we've been doing for the last year. But then we started settling down and taking a lot of these songs that we just made up on the spot, that people seem to like, and just redid them and kept it up, so we have practised a few.'

They all live in a Hollywood home, which they call the Monkey House.

Rathbone's big break was to come when he played Jasper Hale in the big-screen adaptation of the hugely successful book *Twilight*. It was to change his life, but he put his success down to his lucky guitar.

'They were casting for a couple of months, considering different people for different roles. For me, it was fairly simple. The audition place was close to where I live, so I just walked there, with my guitar, for the auditions and two call-backs. The first one, I happened to bring my guitar by pure chance, and then, for the next two, I was like, "Well, I got a call-back from the first one, so I might as well keep bringing my guitar. It might be lucky."

'So, I would just be in the waiting room with all the other actors and they'd be talking and I'd be lightly playing the guitar until I got called.'

When he landed the part, he had no idea what he had let himself in for, since he had never read the books. He revealed, 'I called my parents and let them know I was doing the film, and my mother was like, "Oh, the book *Twilight*, OK." And, she told my little sister, who's thirteen, and all of her friends love the book and were just going gaga over it. And then my family read the books and they just fell in love with them. They burned through the first three within a week or two. And then all my cousins started calling me from all over. They had all found out that I was doing it and they were so excited. That was the first tip to me. I was like, "Wow, people know this book!"

'Everybody loves these stories, and they're beautiful, so it's an honour to be a part of it.'

chapter eight

The Spirited One

'I'm going to book this part, is what's going to happen. I worked my butt off for it.' – Ashley Greene

Like the character that she would be most famous for, Ashley Greene was always bubbly and spirited. 'I always liked performing. I always liked being in front of people,' she told *Interview* magazine. Born on 21 February 1987, Ashley Greene was welcomed into the world by her mother Michele, former US Marine father Joe and brother Joe.

She was an athletic girl at Jacksonville High School, admitting, 'When I was growing up, I cheered and danced and ran and stuff like that. I'm probably thinner now than I was in high school. I had a lot of muscle – a *lot* of muscle – in high school. When I was a kid I did martial arts, and then I did all-star crazy competitive cheer and dance, and then I swam, so I was very muscular. You know, healthy, but not quite as thin as I am.'

As well as cheerleading and tae kwon do – in which she won awards – she took honours classes as well as working as a restaurant hostess. 'I was a pretty good kid,' she said.

She was also very competitive. Greene hates losing to anything. She even took that streak to playing the *Twilight* board game with her co-stars. And, unsurprisingly, she won at that as well ('I don't know if I should be proud of that or not').

Talking about her prom night, she remembered, 'I bought my dress and I pretty much paid for everything because my parents really didn't have the money to pay for something like that. I worked for it, so I think it meant that much more to me because I had to save up.

'I went with my high-school sweetheart and had a blast. I had that fairytale prom everyone talks about.'

She studied law, and loved the studies – maybe not as much as her parents, however, who were delighted with their daughter's plans for adulthood, telling friends, 'Our daughter's going to go to law school or become a psychologist!'

Greene added, 'And then, out of nowhere, I pulled the acting card on them.'

She originally had plans to model for a living but was told she was too small for the catwalk and should focus on getting modelling work on TV adverts. Ironically, it was her law and psychology classes that would sow the seeds of her burgeoning acting talent.

While performing mock trials for class she realised she loved taking centre stage and stating her case.

Buoyed by her enjoyment of performing, she took an acting class. Amazingly, after one class, not only did she know that this was her calling, but she secured a manager!

Recounting the tale, she said, 'And then I went on a trip to New York City and got an agent, at which point my manager and agent told my mom, "She needs to move to LA." I think they were crazy for saying that but I'm so glad that they did.'

She was desperate to prove herself as an actress, and she believed heading to LA was her calling. With her parents' blessing she dropped out of high school to head out to Hollywood, despite there being just one semester left before graduation. She told Jacksonville.com, 'Christmas break, I just kind of left. I didn't really want to highly publicize that, yeah, "I'm going to California to try to become an actress." But it ended up getting around. Nobody can keep anything secret in high school.'

LA was a culture shock to Greene. Her mother, Michele, came down for the first two weeks to see her daughter's place – which she shared with two other aspiring actresses from her town. Her mum sorted out the water and power for the flat, because, as Greene conceded, 'I had no idea what any of that stuff was.'

She used to get so lost going to auditions, she would

phone her mum to look at directions on the computer! Michele remembered, 'It was scary. There were a lot of late nights where we lay in bed and talked about it. But it's kind of a catch-22: If you raise your kid to follow their dreams, you're kind of on the hook.'

Of course, her parents' 'blessing' came with an ultimatum. 'It was more frightening for my mother and father than it was for me. I have a certain way of thinking where I see something, and I know that I want it and I make up my mind – and that's pretty much all there is to it. It was like, this is what I want to do, and I'm going, and everything's going to work out. I'm going to be an actress.

'There was no way around it. My parents, on the other hand… Obviously, they had a lot of long talks and sleepless nights. I was always a good kid, so they went out on a limb. But they did say, "If you go out to LA and start becoming this wild child, then you have to come back home and go to college."'

She told her local paper, 'I think it was more gutsy for my parents than it was for me, it was what I wanted to do; it seemed logical to me. But my parents, for them to think, "Oh yeah, we'll support you doing that at 17" – that was a gutsy move for them. A lot of parents thought they were crazy, but they trusted me.'

She's still incredibly close to her parents – with regular calls lasting through the night to her mother. With a year's rent all being paid for by her parents, and manager and agent all signed up, Greene turned up in

Hollywood hugely excited and confident she could make a career for herself.

And that confidence was justified: she scored her first audition on US soap *Days of Our Lives*. However, the reality of how hard it is to become an actor or actress was to become very clear. Despite having met the producers five times for a role on the soap, she didn't get the part. She would later say, 'They just toyed with me for a little bit.

'I came out to LA all set up, and then I did extremely well in my first audition, so I had this kind of false hope in my mind. You know, everyone says it's really hard, but then you come out and do extremely well the first go. And then reality hits, and it's like nothing, nothing, nothing for a long time.

'There was a time or two where [my parents] were like, "You probably need to come back to Florida." But it just so happened that every time they told me to come home I would coincidentally book some type of role. I don't know if it was fate or luck, and it was just happening at the right time, or if it was that they would say, "You are coming home," and I would immediately go into survival-of-the-fittest mode and book something.

'But, whatever the case, it happened. And I did struggle. I definitely struggled. And I'm always grateful to my parents for letting me struggle, because you really don't appreciate it as much, I don't think, if you don't realise what you're gaining. But they paid my rent for the first year.'

Her brother said, 'I think we all had confidence that she had all the skills and attitude to be one of the people who actually make it out there, that it's something she'd fall into. She's always been a social butterfly – even though she's pretty, she's still real nice.'

She would go on to appear in guest roles in several TV shows such as *Punk'd*, *Crossing Jordan*, *MADtv* and *Shark*. As well as learning her craft, she also found time to be romantically linked to Adrian Grenier, *Lost* star Ian Somerhalder (who, coincidentally, would himself feature in a vampire romp, the TV series *The Vampire Diaries*, playing Damon Salvatore) and *Gossip Girl*'s Chace Crawford. Perhaps it was just a way of making up lost time for Greene. She explained, 'I was a pretty good kid. I didn't really have a boyfriend, really, until I was probably sixteen, which my parents were thrilled about. I was like, "I have no time for boys," and my dad was, "Yes, I think you're right."'

The part of Alice Cullen was something that Greene 'worked my butt off' trying to land. She loved the character of Alice and was desperate to be in the movie. *Twilight* was and still is her favourite book of the series.

Even so, when she finally got the phone call to say she was going to be a member of the Cullen family in the *Twilight* movie, she tried to play it cool, even though in reality she was shaking inside.

'My managers were like, "You're going into a great

casting office. They cast great projects. They're sticklers. If you suck, they won't call you back in." So I was like, "OK, I'll pay extra attention." Then I figured out there wasn't a script or a breakdown, but there was a book. So I got the series and fell in love with it. Then that determination kicked in and I was like, "OK, I'm going to book this part, is what's going to happen." I worked my butt off for it.'

She added to Mediablvd.com, 'I went in for Bella originally. I went in for her two times and met with Catherine Hardwicke, but I wasn't right for that. And then they brought me back in for Alice. I was super-excited. I had read all three books by then because I liked the series so much. And then, I didn't really hear anything. It went really well, and then I went home for Christmas, thinking I hadn't gotten the part. I was upset about it. I cried about it. It was just one of those parts where I was like, "This is my part!" I wanted it, even from when the first time I went in. And then, I ended up getting a call and they were like, "Hey, by the way, you got the part!"'

The first person she told was her dad, who cried at the great news.

Finishing the two weeks' notice at the restaurant that she worked in, Greene got her costume fitted, and then headed to Portland to begin filming for what was to be the role of her life.

chapter nine

Twilight

'When Rob was announced people had a meltdown on the Internet. People said horrible things all over.' – Catherine Hardwicke on the casting of Pattinson as Edward

Summit Entertainment turned to director Catherine Hardwicke to adapt the hugely successful novel by Stephenie Meyer for the big screen. She had already impressed with the handling of the complexities of female teen life in a critically lauded indie film – 2003's *Thirteen*. As soon as Hardwicke got the job she knew straightaway that there was going to be one part that was going to prove incredibly hard to cast.

'Edward was the big problem. How do you find the best-looking guy in the whole world that everyone is going to think is great-looking, but he has to be believable as a seventeen-year-old in high school?

'That takes out almost every hot actor you can think of. They are not high-school boys. And then he has to be pale-skinned, and that eliminates a whole other group. And it's weird, he has to look otherworldly – and so many cute guys came in, but they all looked like you could see them at your high school. Or "Hey, that looks like the guy on our football team" or "He looks like the prom king at our school" – and that's not what you want. You want someone who you believe was not a normal person – who had that special quality and this internal torture.'

Thousands people were looking to play the part of the immortal vampire, but Hardwicke was becoming increasingly frustrated about not getting her man. Too many potential Edwards were just actors who were relying too much on their good looks.

Summit Entertainment chief Erik Feig remembered telling a colleague, ' "I know we've looked. I just feel there are a couple of rocks that we haven't checked under. There have to be British actors that we don't know about that are this guy, who can do a great American accent. Do me a favour. Go to IMDB [Internet Movie Database] and look at every young actor, from age 15 to 25, who was in *Harry Potter* or anything, even a tiny role, print out their headshots."

'I came back from lunch. She had all these pictures, and she said, as we were going through the pictures, "What about this guy?" And I saw a picture of Cedric Diggory. I said, "He's great!" And the look that jumped out to me at that point, and I know it's a silly adjective to use, he was Byronic.'

That Byronic face belonged to Robert Pattinson, of

course, and he was caught in two minds about the part. On the one hand, he was so desperate to land the role that he decided to film an impromptu audition tape with a male friend re-enacting the chemistry class scene where Bella and Edward have their first proper conversation. Unsurprisingly, his attempt at charming his male friend didn't quite compare to the chemistry he would end up having with Kristen Stewart, who would play Bella Swan. In fact the final results embarrassed him so much that he refused to send the tape in. 'It looked so ridiculous,' he said.

In another sense, the more Pattinson thought about it the more he was unsure not only how to play Edward but whether he wanted to play him at all. He believed at the time that Edward was just window dressing and that it was essentially going to be just a modelling job.

But it was a job that Pattinson needed at that stage of his career and, if he wanted to try out for the role of Edward, he would have to spend his own money to fly to America for the audition.

Hardwicke recalled, 'When I talked to [Robert] on the phone in London, at the time he was – as he likes to say – unemployable. He was in between gigs and broke. He took the risk to fly over on his own dime and stay on his agent's couch. She [had] called and said, "Be honest, do you really not have your Edward? I don't want to bring him over here for nothing." I said, "To be honest I don't have it. And I cannot cast

Rob without meeting the person and seeing how he works with Kristen. This is all about chemistry."'

And there would certainly be chemistry. The audition scene between Pattinson and Stewart would go on to become one of Hollywood's most bizarre ones – with both being asked to play out an intimate scene on Hardwicke's bed.

Hardwicke told MTV, 'They came to my house – they had just met. I said, "I know you just met, but I need you to do this scene. We're gonna do it in my bedroom, on the bed – and you're really gonna kiss."

'Kristen already had to kiss three other guys that day. She was kind of sleepy and just hanging out – and then Robert appeared in the room. His hair was a little different – it was his Dalí hair, with the black bangs.

'He was a bit nervous, because suddenly you've just met a girl and you're going to start making out with the person – and someone is filming. [He] was really wild on the first take – use your imagination.

'I had to tell him, "This is going to be a PG-13 movie!" and have him settle down a little bit. Afterwards, Kristen and I were looking at each other like, "Whoa!"

'They had to do it three times. The first time, they went a little too far, and I was like, "I can't show this to anybody at the studio!" After we finished the whole thing and we had met bachelors one, two, three and four. It had to be Rob. She basically threatened me.'

Stewart told *GQ*, 'Everybody came in doing

something empty and shallow and thoughtless. I know that's a f**king great thing to say about all the other actors – but Rob understood that it wasn't a frivolous role.'

Foreshadowing the chemistry between the pair that would become intently scrutinised by both the fans and the worldwide media, Hardwicke recalled, 'What Rob and Kristen had is a multitude of feelings for each other. Complex feeling for each other. It was what we needed. Complex, intense fascination.'

If Pattinson was intense at the audition, it was partly because he was having panic attacks before it took place and ended up taking the anxiety-combating drug Valium in a bid to ease his nerves.

Talking to *GQ*, he said, 'It was the first time I've ever taken Valium. I tried to do it for another audition, and it just completely backfired – I was passing out.'

In fact, he was so convinced that he had embarrassed himself during the audition that he phoned his parents, telling them 'That's it.' However, Pattinson remembered their saying, '"Ok… fine," which was not the answer I wanted to hear.'

It's hard to believe now, but Pattinson's casting was met with fury from a lot of *Twilight* fans. Like Nikki Reed (see Chapter 6), Pattinson was also seen as the wrong choice by the fans.

Reflecting to *Time* magazine in 2009, Hardwicke said, 'When Rob was announced people had a meltdown on the Internet. People said horrible things all over. There were a few pictures of him by the paparazzi that were in London, walking out of a club, not having shaved, looking like a slob.

'I said to Rob, "As soon as we get your look down and get your photos out I know you're going to be good. You just have to have faith. This happens to a lot of actors." One day he came to me and said, "I got this email forwarded to me about how revolting I am." I said, "Rob, you cannot read these things. Don't torture yourself." And he said, "I didn't. My mother forwarded that to me."'

Talking about the negative reaction, Pattinson recalled, to *Entertainment Weekly*, 'I stopped reading [them] after I saw the signature saying, "Please, anyone else."'

Producer Greg Mooradian recalled of the casting process, 'On the fan websites, every single person who read the book had already cast the film for you twenty times over. We did take a look at their ideas and we decided we were never going to please everybody, so what we had to do was go with our guts. The actors we cast are the actors we feel best embodied these characters.

'It took forever to cast this movie, but once we found Bella and all of the Cullens, I realised we finally had it. When I actually got to see them together performing in a scene, it took my breath away.'

Hardwicke remembered, however, that selling Pattinson to the studio had its difficulties. 'He was dishevelled. He was a different weight. His hair was different and dyed black (from his *Little Ashes* role). He was all sloppy. The studio head said, "You want to cast this guy as Edward Cullen?" I said, "Yeah." And he said, "Do you think you can make him look good?" I said, "Yes, I do."

'So I said, "Here's what I'm going to do. I'm going to get his hair back to a different colour, do a different style. He would work with a trainer from now on. My cinematographer is great with lighting. He will study the cheekbones, and I promise you, we'll make this guy look good."'

Summit announced in February 2008, 'Finding [seven] talented actors who can portray supernaturally beautiful, talented vampires of the sort Stephenie Meyer has created and her fans have come to know and love was not an easy task. But we are happy to say we have found our perfect Cullen family.'

The Cullens were cast, and Lutz has credited the film's director for her choices.

He told *Teen Dream*, 'Well, I really think Catherine did an amazing job with casting people who are similar to their characters and talented, but really, what it comes down to is that we are all really down to earth and have a great head on our shoulders.

'So it is really nice for all of us to stay humble and not get "ego tripped" with everything that comes with the success of *Twilight* and the fans who have shown so much love and support. We are just a great group of actors and we're real and we're down to earth and it's great to have that camaraderie and hang out on and off set in Vancouver, LA or Portland. It is a really close knit family.'

The actors who played the Cullen family would become incredibly close, with some of them reverting to their character types.

Peter Facinelli admits that he ended up becoming a somewhat patriarchal figure during the film. 'And it was weird because I used to be the youngest one on the set, and this was one of my first projects where I was one of the oldest ones on the set. And that's pretty rare. I guess I'm becoming older. It's a blink of an eye and suddenly I'm the dad.

'But it was great working with Kristen Stewart, Rob Pattinson and the other younger actors. Especially the newer actors. They have this energy and they're not jaded yet. So they have this freshness and spontaneity. And they all started calling me dad, which was funny.'

Hardwick called the chemistry between the pair as soon as they walked on the set 'extremely intense right away'. But the chemistry wasn't reserved just for the leading man and the leading lady. 'There were emotional roller coasters going on between various cast members the whole time,' said Hardwicke. 'So that's pretty wild. You have this hot, young, cute, sexy cast and you're out of town at hotels. It's going to happen. How do you keep people focused on the work so that nothing else gets in the way? That's the trick. Rob and

Kristen and all the cast members wanted to do a good job. This was a cool opportunity.'

Kellan Lutz added, 'As far as with Nikki Reed and myself, I hadn't really hung out with her [in the past], so it was my mission, as well as hers, to make the relationship of Rosalie and Emmett, and be able to portray a realness on screen. We're married and we pretend to be siblings, so we had to feel each other out and know the quirkiness of it all. So, we'd hang out and go to dinner all the time, and we built puzzles and just did random stuff.

'The cast would all hang out off the set because we were all around the same age range and it was such a great cast to work with. Everyone was really cool. We'd all go to dinner, or go to the bar next door and listen to the bands play, and just relax.'

While they became all friends on set, Pattinson would withdraw himself slightly from them. As with the process he went through for *Little Ashes*, he was desperate to immerse himself into the character.

'Right after the audition, I found myself bizarrely invested in the story and I hadn't even read the books at that point. I've gotten more attached to it. '

To get the right physical shape needed for the role he hired a personal trainer, because, as Hardwicke noted, 'He's a Brit and they hit the pubs all the time. They don't take too kindly to gyms. And he did work out with a trainer. He was very diligent. If they did four hours of work, he would do an extra hour on his own.

I was like, "Rob your body wants to exercise; your muscles want to be used."'

Robert added, 'I got injured on the first shot of the first day. I wasn't even doing a stunt. I was just trying to pick up Kristen, and I almost tore my hamstring because I hadn't been doing enough squats. It was very embarrassing.'

Pattinson was being somewhat bashful, as Chaske Spencer, who plays the werewolf Sam in *New Moon*, confirmed when he said that the actor was something of a dark horse when it came to working out. During filming of the movie, Pattinson in fact set the record on a rowing-machine competition.

There were other mishaps on set, with Nikki Reed so desperate to prove to the series' fans that she was the right person to play Rosalie, that she bleached her hair. However, her hair ended up falling out as a result. For *New Moon* and subsequent films in the series she will now use a wig.

However, *Twilight* was an opportunity that Pattinson was desperate to take seriously. He believed that the way to achieve the otherworldly feeling that Edward didn't belong was to make sure that he didn't get too close to the cast.

Speaking to Moviehole.net, he said, 'I didn't talk to any of the cast about anything other than the film for at least a month and a half of the shoot. And it creates a strange aura around you, and people don't really know what to make of you. I just wanted the rest of the cast to think about me as a character being this intense person.'

Rest time between shots would see Pattinson laze out in the background with a book in his hand or he would stare intently at the dailies (rushes) of each shot, desperate to make sure that he had found the character on screen. And he retained the intensity even with the author of the book series, Stephenie Meyer.

'I was talking to Stephenie Meyer saying the guy must be chronically depressed,' revealed Pattinson. 'And she was saying, "No, he's not, he's not." But I still maintained that he was. I mean, it's not like depressed, but just this sort of loneliness. I mean, when you see him at school, he doesn't really talk to anyone. He must get bored after a while only hanging out with the same four people in his life.'

Meyer waded into the debate, explaining, 'With Rob, we sat before the filming started. It wasn't an argument but we did actually disagree on his character. I'd be like "No this is how it is." He's like, "No, it's definitely this way." Yet in the performance he did what he wanted, and yet it was exactly what I wanted.'

She added to *Entertainment Weekly*, 'He's a very mesmerising person to be around. He's got such a compelling personality. I don't think you'd want him for a boyfriend. And you couldn't just be his friend because he's terribly sexy!'

Despite that debate, Meyer entrusted Robert with something very valuable indeed. To get more into character, he was given a sneak peak of, at that time, one of the most eagerly awaited publishing events in recent years – *Midnight Sun*, a novel that retells the story of *Twilight* from Edward's point of view. (It has now been abandoned until further notice after the first handful of chapters were leaked on the Internet. Pattinson jokingly insists *he* didn't do it!)

'I am definitely the only person apart from her and the editor who has read it,' he told *MTV* at the time. 'Just me and Catherine. It is very top-secret. And it is like halfway, two-thirds finished. I read that right at the beginning [of filming]. I got a lot of stuff out of that.

'It's exactly the same events, but a couple of other things happen. You get the same gist, but it's funny how different things affect Edward in ways that you don't really expect if you have just read *Twilight*.

'I knew that the first chapter existed and I based a lot of my angst from that on the character. It's talking about how little control he has. In the book it seems that when he says, "I'm a monster and I'm going to kill you," and she says "I'm not afraid," you kind of know the whole time in the book that he's never going to do anything bad. But you read the first chapter of *Midnight Sun*, where the full extent of how much he wanted to kill her, and how he's considering killing the entire school just so that he can kill her, becomes evident.

'I wanted that element of him to be very prominent. I wanted Bella to be saying "I'm not scared, you won't do anything to me," but not with such certainty. So that it would suddenly be like, "You won't do anything to me – will you?" I kind of wanted something like that. I think it makes it sexier if there's a very real chance of him just flipping out and killing her.'

What surprised him, however, was that it turns out he had understood the character more than he realised.

'[It turned out] we had the same perspective!'

As we have seen, *Midnight Sun* was shelved after the first few chapters were leaked onto the Internet, with an upset Meyer claiming in a terse statement that the book was over.

However, she has since said that the statement, which included the line, 'If I wrote it now everybody would end up dying' – was 'kind of tongue-in-cheek'. And she has since spoken about working on it again.

Despite the heated discussion between Pattinson and Meyer, his intensity actually helped lighten the mood on set – with the cast and crew bonding over their mischievous aim to try to get the serous actor to laugh. They would follow him around, reciting passages of the book that showed the lighter aspects of Edward – an element of the character that he tried to steer away from as much as possible.

But it wasn't just Pattinson who was the victim of on-set banter. Lutz is a serial prankster, admitting, 'I like to scare the girls – just hiding behind a door, all you have to do is grab their leg, and there goes the coffee.'

Facinelli revealed, 'Edi Gathegi [Laurent in *Twilight*

and *New Moon*] was the biggest joker. He does all these voices, so he would call me [on the phone] and pretend like he was different people. Like, he called my room and said he was some girl named Suzie, and I was like, "Who is this?" One day I told him to call Jackson Rathbone and do Suzie for him and say he was Suzie from the production office. So he called and said, "Hey, this is Suzie from the production office. We just want to tell you that we're dying your hair back to brown, because we don't like blond hair!" '

But Hardwicke admits she found Pattinson's self-doubt challenging to channel in the film.

Talking to About.com, she remarked, 'Whenever we tried to rehearse a scene or shoot a scene, he would get one line out and then just stop and second-guess himself, and, like, hate the line, hate everything he's doing. And I'd be like, "You know, I actually thought you were doing pretty well. Why don't we just go through the whole scene and then look at it in the big picture, OK?"

'He would do two lines and stop and I'd be like, "Oh my God, I have five seconds to get this right. I have five minutes to get things right." I don't want to say that but, "Rob, OK, that was great, we got two lines. Let's do the whole scene this time and don't second-guess yourself. Don't stop." I mean, "Please God, do the whole scene." And then finally when he would do it I'd go, "Hey that was actually pretty damn good, Rob. It's good. Here's a little note. Here's a little note…" And finally if I could just get him to do it, it would work.

'I've never had an actor like Rob or Kristen. They are remarkable, but they are definitely challenging in a way. Or, because they're challenging everything in themselves, too, not just me. They were trying to find it and they were trying to make it really great.'

Remarking on Pattinson's performance as Edward, Oliver Irving, director of *How To Be*, said, '[Robert's] not this slick, well-oiled, Disneyfied person. In *Twilight* his character is like the most perfect person, but there's something about his performance that shows little bits of awkwardness and his inner feelings.'

And Pattinson was certainly feeling awkward: in one scene in which Edward kisses Bella in her bedroom he got too passionate and promptly fell off the bed!

One of the big moments in the book was of course the famed vampire baseball scene. Facinelli, a former baseball star in his younger days, declined a stuntman for his scenes. 'I didn't have to do that much. All I had to do was slide into second base, which they actually gave me a stunt double for but I told them, "I think I can handle this." So I practised. It was supposed to be a super slide so I jumped off a little mini tramp[oline] and so it was fun. I like doing stunts, stunts are fun for me. I try to do as many of them as I can. During the slide I bruised up my leg pretty bad.'

Speaking before the film's release, Facinelli highlighted the vampire baseball scene as one to watch:

'I mean, you can only do so much with your imagination, when you're thinking about vampire baseball and reading the book. But actually seeing that and hearing the cracking of the bat? The super-vampire speed? That should be fun to watch.'

There's a moving flashback scene in the movie, which sees Peter Facinelli's character Carlisle 'turning' Edward into a vampire. The scene is meant to show Carlisle's reluctance to place such a burden on the young Edward but that he has no other choice, as he doesn't want Edward to die.

Facinelli thought it would be a good idea to whisper something into Robert's ear when he bites him – an intimate moment that only the two of them would hear. However, Facinelli revealed not only what he said but also how it would be something different each take.

He started whispering, 'I'm sorry', then, 'Be reborn, my son.' But after a few of these takes he started messing around by saying, 'Rob, you're so sexy.' Amazingly, Facinelli insisted that the reaction shown on the film is from that line!

At the end of the shoot it became clear to Pattinson how close they had all become. When filming had finished (it was at the scene in which Edward drives Bella back to her dad after their date at a restaurant), Robert went back to his trailer to chill out. Putting on a video, he suddenly burst into tears. It was then that he knew how important this film had been to him.

Kellan Lutz and Ashley Greene in particular became incredibly close. They knew each other before, but *Twilight* had really bonded them. 'I can tell anything and everything to her.' Elizabeth Reaser and Nikki Reed, meanwhile, could often be found on set 'scampering around, finding snacks and making fun of each other' – according to Reaser. Reed claims that the pair both helped themselves to each other's snacks in their trailers.

To remember her time on *Twilight*, Greene kept a memento. 'I have the band that Jasper gave Alice. I've had it on since the first film and haven't given it back.'

Although the book's fanbase was huge, it wasn't a given that the success of the book would translate at the box office. '*Sisterhood of the Traveling Pants*, that was successful but it made $30 million with this kind of fanbase,' said Hardwicke.

Facinelli, however, was quick to big the film up to excite the fanbase (not that they needed much encouragement!).

'Over five hundred pages are in the book, so you can't fit every single detail in. And some details will be different. Stephenie Meyer is very detail-oriented, to the point where she describes clothes in the scene! So, sometimes it's not going to be as detailed or as specific as the book. There will be subtle differences, but the essence is there.'

The film, which cost more than $37 million to make, grossed more than $200 million in the US alone, and another $160 million in DVD sales. The soundtrack sold 2.2 million copies.

The success came as no surprise for Pattinson, who had an inkling that *Twilight* would be a huge box-office hit.

'I don't really think even the production company knew how big it was going to become. It's interesting, but as we were shooting it sort of got bigger and bigger and bigger, and more and more people started turning up to the set every day.'

Facinelli, however, had no idea, explaining, 'When we first shot it, you know, I think no one really knew that it was going to be this big. I think we were just hoping to satisfy the fans of the books, and we knew there was this underground following. Again, no one really knew it was going to snowball into this huge thing.'

But snowball it did, and, if the cast didn't know how big the film would become, they soon would.

chapter ten
Twilight Success

'A mother recently gave me her baby and asked me,
"Can you please bite her head?"' – Robert Pattinson

With *Twilight* scoring a huge success at the box office (it took more than $70 million in its first three days, a staggering figure for a modestly budgeted movie), it blasted the film's main characters to superstardom – particularly Pattinson.

When he had been cast, Meyer remembered asking the studio bosses, 'Is Rob ready for this? Have you guys prepped him? Is he ready to be the *it* guy? I don't think he really is.'

Whether or not Robert had any idea then of how much things were going to change, he very much knew after a trip to the DVD rental store Blockbuster.

'I had forgotten it was being released that day. There were two families who had come with eight- or nine-year-old daughters to get their DVD. They were standing in the line crying and I stood watching what all this commotion was about. They didn't know I was there or anything. I was just thinking, "Wow, you're crying about a DVD." It's fascinating.'

A couple of incidents left a burning impression on him.

'A mother recently gave me her baby and asked me, "Can you please bite her head!"' he told *OK!* magazine. Another incident saw him being accosted by four women who 'had scratches and scabs into the side of their necks, so it was freshly bleeding when they came up to get a signature. They were like, "We did this for you." I didn't know what to say. I was like, "Gross!"'

And he's not the only one.

'You get the, "Can you bite me?" a lot,' said Facinelli. 'Once in a while I'll bite them on the wrist for a picture. It's fun, you know.'

Pattinson also revealed the lengths that fans have gone to in order to get a glimpse of their idol. 'People ambush me and try to figure out what hotel I'm staying at, as well as wanting to touch my hair. Everyone just screams and screams. It still feels surreal.'

Another incident saw a fan hospitalised after she got into a fight with another fan over copies of a limited-edition poster of Pattinson that were handed out a premiere of the Pattinson DVD documentary *Robsessed*.

Apart from Pattinson, Stewart and now Taylor Lautner (who plays the werewolf Jacob), the rest of the cast have been able to dip in and out of the worldwide buzz whenever they like. They can sample the crazy, heady atmosphere without having to live the day-to-day attention that the main stars receive.

Facinelli explained, 'I didn't get as much recognition from the first movie, which is kind of nice. I could walk down the street and get a cup of coffee, but Rob couldn't go anywhere. He had to go into hiding.'

However, he has begun to notice that he gets more and more fans. Not that his family are impressed. 'I co-coach my daughters' soccer team, and if someone comes over to ask for an autograph, they roll their eyes.'

Nikki Reed says of the *Twilight* fans, 'They're the sweetest people.'

That's not to say that they're strangers to a bizarre autograph scenario every once in a while.

Said Facinelli, 'I was in Hawaii floating on the deck, lying in the sun, and I had my two-year-old daughter napping on my shoulder. Some girl swam out there and asked, "Are you Dr Carlisle?" it was really funny.'

Facinelli added, 'I feel for Robert. He didn't sign up for this knowing what it would become. The fanbase has grown ever since we filmed it. There were underground fans when we started. I remember we'd all go to their website and they said, "All these actors are wrong for the roles. Facinelli doesn't have blond hair. What are they thinking?" For Rob, he just signed up thinking it'd be a cool little movie. All of a sudden he's like the James Dean of today.

'That's a lot to put on a guy's shoulders, but

hopefully he'll be OK. He's kind of nerve-racked. He doesn't like to leave his apartment a lot. But I think it'll be good. This will bring good things to him.'

Asked if he could give advice for Pattinson on how to deal with the fame, he told *Radar Online*, 'I don't think there's any advice to be given. It's a learning curve. Even for me, I've been working for 15 years and I've never had the kind of fanbase this movie has.

'People always come up to me and said they like me in my old movies, but with a movie like this when I walk somewhere people's faces actually drop when they see me or fans will scream when they see us. That takes some getting used to; I wish someone would give me some advice. If people are watching, what are you going to do with that? You turn it around and try to do positive things like work with the Make-A-Wish Foundation. I feel very lucky to be able to do that.' (He has played baseball for the foundation and is a supporter.)

Christian Serratos, who plays Angela Weber, Bella's classmate, recalled, 'The last time I went out with Kristen, Rob Pattinson and Ashley Greene, it took Rob almost an entire hour longer to get there because it took him so long to get out of the hotel.'

Greene, however, admitted that she suffered a nervous breakdown following the immediate success of *Twilight*. Before the franchise she was a jobbing actress. One film later, she was suddenly a role model to millions of teenage girls.

She was also mortified to discover personal nude photos she took of herself before she found fame on *Twilight* were leaked onto the Internet.

She told *Interview* magazine, 'There was a moment in time where I was kind of having this mini-breakdown because it was all very new, and it was all being thrown at me really quickly, and I was going, "Why are people reporting on this?"

'Why do people care what I'm wearing or what I'm eating, and why are people looking down on me because I'm not wearing high heels?

'That's the downside to being in the public eye. When girls come up and say, "You're my role model," it's really flattering, but it's also really scary because I'm not perfect and I'm going to make mistakes.

'I've just decided that I have to continue to live my life and do what I do. Hopefully, people love me because of who I am, not who I pretend to be.'

Pattinson said, 'I'd like to think that I haven't changed that much. Within myself I don't think I've changed. I think I look down a lot more. It's kind of extraordinary. I don't think any of us expected any of this to happen, and especially that the franchise seems to keep building and building. It's just gotten bigger and bigger. It's an interesting thing to deal with.'

How he will deal with it is anyone's guess. Even after the success of *New Moon*, the actor still doesn't have a publicist. He said, 'My manager always tells me,

"Robert, you really need a publicist." And I say, "Oh, but you're doing such a great job with the publicity!"'

Kristen Stewart joked in an interview, 'His manager has to work ten times harder.'

The *Twilight* series is something of both a blessing and a curse for Pattinson – with him longing for the days of going out in public without finding himself swarmed by the press and fans.

In an interview with *Entertainment Weekly*, the journalist recalled the time he and Pattinson wandered into a Hollywood bar without any attention. When told of the moment, Pattinson said, 'That was a different world. I miss that so much. The idea of an interview now, unaccompanied, and saying, "Hey, let's go to a bar…" Jesus Christ, I'd have so many [studio] people on my ass.'

Peter Facinelli tries to make sure, however, that things don't change too much for the sake of his family. Facinelli dotes on them, and, even with the success of *Twilight*, he and Garth are determined to make sure that they still go about their normal lives. He even took them on a West Coast road trip when he was asked to compete in a charitable Vampire Baseball tournament.

With Garth cooking eggs and bacon in their motor vehicle, and Facinelli in the driving seat, you could easily mistake one of one Hollywood's most rising stars for a normal family man. Facinelli does admit, however, that he's a better actor than driver: 'I got four tickets in three weeks, all for different things. I was some kind of police magnet, I don't know why. I'm going to fight all of them; you never want to admit you're wrong. I should go there in person and fight all of them.'

Twilight's success also proved a vindication for Nikki Reed, who was hurt by criticisms of her casting long before the cameras rolled. And she has now revealed that she gets on famously with the *Twilight* fans.

'There's a Nikki Reed mafia group that shows up to events to make sure that nobody is mean to me.'

Talking about the fan attention, Elizabeth Reaser noted, 'Not much has changed. It's been different up here in Vancouver – there have been a lot of fans. I'm a very private person, and I've never had that much interaction on the street. So that's been a whole different experience for me.'

But, if the Cullen actors thought it was crazy following the success of *Twilight*, *New Moon* was set to ramp it up a notch.

New Moon

'I liked doing Twilight, *but it felt very much like an indie movie – and* New Moon *definitely feels like it's a big movie.'* – Robert Pattinson

The sequel to *Twilight* was quickly green-lit following the huge media attention of the first film. One reason was to capitalise on the success of *Twilight* and to appease the fans' demands. The other reason was more practical. For a series that features young-looking vampires who don't age, it would look a bit silly if the films were two or three years apart.

The main problem for the follow-up was somehow to get more screen time for Pattinson's Edward Cullen – not that he was becoming a diva, but more because the character is absent for a large portion of the book.

'When you look at the book, you wonder, "How is this going to work?"' pondered Hardwicke, shortly before Chris Weitz replaced her as director. 'That's one of the balancing acts that are being considered. It's definitely an issue, because we all love that chemistry between Rob and Kristen, but that's also what's great about *New Moon* – he has to break himself away from [Bella], and the depression she gets into, the deep depression. That is the whole story, and you have to keep the integrity.'

The angle she was keen to play was to abandon the story from Bella's eyes. 'That could be one of the ways,' she told *MTV*. 'Though, his story was a little bit depressing, it seems like he just sat down in a room and [sulked]. But, you can always make that interesting.'

Indeed, the absence of Pattinson was a nightmare for the film's bosses. It took them ages to find their screen hunk after a long casting process, and he's hardly in the second book!

What Weitz and screenwriter Melissa Rosenberg concocted was to have him appear in both Bella dream sequences and in the apparitions she has every time she attempts something dangerous.

Despite his lack of screen time, *New Moon* is Robert's favourite book of the series, 'mainly because I like the juxtaposition. Edward is such a hyped character, and there are so many people looking at him like a romantic hero. In *New Moon*, the way that I read it anyway, he's just so humbled.

'It's a character who's looking at Bella and thinking that he loves something too much, but he can't be around her. He deliberately starts breaking up their relationship, which I think is a very relatable thing that can be very painful.'

With Chris Weitz taking over from Hardwicke for this second film, there could have been some fears that maybe the cast would struggle with a new director taking over the series. However, those fears were unfounded. According to Pattinson, 'Aesthetically, it looks very different. The script was very different. It's a completely different mood. So I'm really interested to see how it works out.

'Catherine has such a specific style and such a specific atmosphere. It's a completely different mood in this one. Chris is great. I really like Chris. It's such a different film. I mean Catherine has a kind of purity about her and a kind of completely uncynical viewpoint about the world. And I think Chris is a little bit cynical and sort of looks at things in a little bit of a darker way. I think this a darker movie.'

Stewart added, 'Chris was the perfect guy to do this movie. Catherine was impulsive and fast. This time we had more time to think. We could be a little more cerebral. And, considering what I had to go through in the movie, he's one of the most compassionate, considerate people I've ever met. He made it so easy.'

Weitz replaced Hardwicke amid reports that Summit Entertainment were so keen to get a sequel under way that they were pushing ahead with the release. Hardwicke had strong opinions herself on how the second one should look and was so burnt out from the first one that she wanted to spend more time on the story rather than heading straight onto the second one.

She released a statement, saying, 'I am sorry that due to timing I will not have the opportunity to direct *New Moon*. Directing *Twilight* has been one of the great experiences of my life, and I am grateful to the fans for their passionate support of the film. I wish everyone at Summit the best with the sequel – it is a great story.'

Summit's co-chairman, Rob Friedman, however, told *Deadline*, 'Catherine and Summit have agreed to part ways on the sequel because our visions are different.'

There were certainly discussions between Hardwicke and the studio bosses during shooting on the film. It was originally expected to shoot for 50 days (a fairly short shooting schedule for that kind of film), and Hardwicke was stunned when they wanted to shorten it.

'It was only 44 days, when we first had 50, and then one day they just came to me and said – they first said, "You cannot do this in 50 days. We don't believe you're going to get your movie made." And, "How can you convince us you can actually do it in 50 days?"

'They said, "For the budget and the amount of money we have, you've only got 50 days to shoot." So I said, "OK, I will find a way to do it. I will do it." And then two days later they came and said, "Now you're having 44 days." I said, "Wait a minute. You just told me that I couldn't do it in 50." I was kind of like, "Wow, I don't understand it." And they were just looking at me like, "Now you have to do it in 44." I'm like, "Am I on another planet?"'

The loss of six days of shooting meant that certain parts of the script would have to be excised, and in actual fact it was the action scenes that were first to go at the behest of the studio, claims Hardwicke.

'They actually made me cut a lot of action. I said, "I think this movie needs action," and I had more cool ideas in the baseball and more in the ballet that I thought would have even ramped it up one more level. But at that moment in time, and this is very weird to think of right now, they said, "We don't care if this goes beyond the core girls. We're not looking for boys. We just want it to be OK for boys, not embarrassing for boys to see it." Now, after they saw all the action and everything, now it's all about getting the boys. But, at that moment in time, they convinced me that they didn't care about boys. But I was the one fighting. "I want action!" I'm like, "Girls like action too."

'But it's been a journey for them too, for Summit. It's a new company and they didn't really know that much about what's going on. You know, everybody was struggling to figure it out. Like, "What do we do?"'

Weitz admitted that he understood why fans of the series were hesitant about his involvement, saying, 'There was a reasonable amount of scepticism when I took over the second movie. I understand that. I directed *American Pie*. I would be worried too.'

Luckily for him, a two-and-a-half-hour phone call with Meyer earned him her blessing. It just so happened that another film he had co-directed with his brother Paul, *About a Boy*, was one of Meyer's favourite films.

Talking about his vision for the film, he said, 'I wanted it to look more old-fashioned than the first movie. Hardwicke's film was very contemporary, very stylish. Very immediate. That was great. But not me. I'm a bit of an old fogey. What I wanted was wide-screen epic.'

Pattinson noted, 'There's definitely a difference in scale. I liked doing *Twilight*, but it felt very much like an indie movie – and *New Moon* definitely feels like it's a big movie.'

While it was most certainly a bigger film, Pattinson called it the 'most relaxing job I've ever done'. And it seemed a description that most people on the film would agree with.

The film's screenwriter Melissa Rosenberg added, '*New Moon* was one of the happiest sets I have ever been on. The [driver] who picked me up said, "This is a great set. Chris Weitz is a genius. It is so wonderful." I was, "OK, dude, you are overselling." But I got on the set and it was just delightful. You can tell when it is uncomfortable and there is no connection. Chris Weitz is just a Zen master. I went to him and I was, "You are so cool and calm. And everyone is so cool and calm."

'He said, "You have no idea what it is going to cost me."

'My husband is a director and I know what it costs

him,' she explained. 'You have to tamp down every ounce of panic and frustration in order to project this calmness. I hope Chris got a good vacation between production and post [-production].'

Weitz would the indeed be the calm guiding hand amid the storm, often wearing a T-shirt with the words 'KEEP CALM AND CARRY ON' emblazoned on the front. And he would need that attitude with the crazy fan attention that the film attracted. The Italy shoot in particular, for the scenes involving the Volturi, attracted a large number of fans.

'Kellan Lutz and I look at each other and go, "What is going on?"' said Ashley Greene, adding, 'We were in this tiny little town and there were fans that flew in from all over, and it got a little crazy.

'It's very different from anything that I've ever experienced. But the fans are so passionate. Seriously, this is the coolest job in the world with the best fans.

'I want to go back! We were in the countryside – you could take a picture and it was a postcard. The place that we stayed in was private, seven villas, and the people who owned it cooked us breakfast, lunch and dinner every day and were just really cool. Even going to work where we were filming – there weren't built sets – it was crazy to be able to go into these incredibly old, gorgeous buildings.'

The actors admitted that meeting up on set again for this second movie was as happy a reunion as you can get.

Rathbone revealed, 'Whenever we got back to film *New Moon*, the first day I was back, the cast was hanging out in Peter Facinelli's room and it was just like a family reunion.

'It was like we'd been away for a month; it didn't seem like a year. It was just really nice to kind of get back together and have that family environment. In terms of having a new director, nothing really changed too much. It was just a different subtle vibe, because the director manages the energy on set. It was great. We all wanted to come together and make another great piece of art for the fans. It's really about what they want to see, because they're the ones buying the tickets.'

Said Facinelli, 'We like to be around each other. We hang out a lot together after work. For me it's very much like a family. I like being with them and I like when we're all together, especially when we're all in scenes together; that's always fun. It's a good cast; it's a good bunch of people. We all like each other, so that's important.'

Twilight's huge success created something of a siege mentality for the cast. They were experiencing the sort of widespread hysteria that comes along only every once in a while, resulting in a situation that has bonded them for life.

When asked if she had feelings for any of her co-stars, Greene said, 'It's funny, though – once you get to know them, you don't think of them in that way.

And Taylor's only seventeen! I'm like, "Are you joking dude? Seventeen-year-olds do not have bodies like that!"

'I see him more as my little brother than a love interest. With Rob I can definitely see the appeal. He's very talented and I think talent makes a guy sexy.

'We all kind of flirt with each other. We share this intense bond. But Jackson and I immediately got along. He was teaching me how to do this stupid dance on the first day I met him! He's adorable.'

Not that the Cullen cast don't have their 'grumpy' moments. Greene told *Vanity Fair*, 'We've gotten to know each other, we've been thrown together, and we're working together six days a week, 12 hours a day. So we've definitely gotten to know each other better, and there's a lot of real chemistry.

'There are also days when you know someone's grumpy! There's one big thing that we can all relate to, and that is how all of our lives have changed drastically. We can rely on each other a little bit more. If someone's going through something, there's someone else in the cast who has gone through something or who is going through the same thing. It's nice.'

There is one thing that bonds the *Twilight* cast more than ever – music. When filming in Vancouver they were regularly spotted at local gigs – whether it was watching the best of the new bands around or one of the Cullens himself on stage.

Rathbone's band, 100 Monkeys, played a gig in

Vancouver during filming of *New Moon* and the cast, crew and author Meyer turned up to support him. They were left incredibly impressed by Rathbone's ability.

'Jackson Rathbone can really play guitar!' wowed Meyer.

Even those who weren't so musically talented still wanted to play a part, it seems. Facinelli told *MTV*, 'You know, I keep telling him I want to dance in the banana suit. He has a guy that dances in a banana suit, and I said, "Can I come to your concert and dance in the banana suit?" I have no musical inclination at all – but I can dance in a banana suit like nobody's business.'

Pattinson is also a hugely talented musician, playing guitar and piano, as well as being equipped with a fine and distinctive singing voice.

Two of his songs, 'Never Think' and 'Let Me Sign', featured in *Twilight*, although it has to be said that he was somewhat reluctant to put them in the film for fear of a backlash from fans thinking it was a cynical exercise.

'That's what I was scared about: it looks like I'm trying to get a music career out of *Twilight* or something. I've never really recorded anything – I just played in pubs and stuff – and I really didn't want it to look like I was trying to cash in. I hope it doesn't come across as that. I'm not going to be doing any music videos or anything.'

Rathbone revealed, 'Rob Pattinson and Kristen and

Nikki would do a lot of jam sessions, and Kellan Lutz and Ashley Greene and Peter Facinelli would all hang out in the hotel room and play music and hang out on the set.'

When they weren't attending music concerts, they would head over to Peter's house for some poker sessions. And when they went to Italy they regularly dined out at the best pizza restaurants in Montepulciano. The Vancouver shoot once again saw mass fan hysteria. However, Pattinson had a cunning plan up his sleeve. Or should that be hood?

'It's the only city in the world where hoods are not fashionable. If you're wearing a hood, you're going to mug people. So I wore a hood, and then I'd sort of spit on the ground a little bit and do a little bit of shaking around as you're walking. Everyone moved to the other side of the street!'

The scenes set in Italy feature the Volturi clan – with acclaimed British actor Michael Sheen playing the clan's leader, Aro.

Sheen said, 'If I'm doing something that's based on a book, then I'll definitely read the book. I look for anything that will give a little clue or something, a little help, a little hint... just things like that. Like one word that Stephenie uses in the book will kind of tee off my imagination.

'Stephenie describes his voice as quite feathery – that's what gave me the idea of making it very soft, and light. I think she describes it as being like a sigh, his voice. And that he's a bit like a concerned grandfather at times, with Edward. I like the idea... even though he's this kind of deadly, really dangerous character, there's something quite sentimental about him, quite soft, and yet the next moment he could eat you.'

While the Cullen clan didn't feature hugely in *New Moon*, Greene's character is an integral part of the story.

'It was incredible, and I think the timing was right. I'm glad that [my role] wasn't that big in the first one because I was wide-eyed and nervous. By the second one, I had the time to fully develop this character, and I'm really comfortable with Alice Cullen now,' said Greene.

Facinelli jokingly moaned about his character, 'I wish that he didn't disappear so much. I would have had him go to Italy and do more. He knows all the Volturi and he could have helped smooth things over. Maybe had a cappuccino with them and said, "Hey, you know, this isn't cool." And I don't want to give it away for people who haven't read the fourth book, but, like any typical doctor when the baby is due, he's not there. He's off on the ninth hole somewhere playing golf; I was like, "What's going on?"'

However, one of the stand-out scenes in *New Moon* featured the Cullen clan and a bemused Bella at her surprise birthday party.

Greene told *Vanity Fair*, 'But filming one of the first scenes, where Alice throws this party and Bella gets a paper cut, was really fun because we were all there. It was basically me and four or five other cast members. The Cullen family was really only there for a week. It was nice because we started out with coming back, reuniting and seeing everyone again... and we got to see Jasper in action.'

Rathbone recalled the scene: 'In a house where we were shooting a very dramatic birthday party scene, the owners were very concerned about their hardwood floors. So the entire crew and entire cast had to wear these hospital scrub-like bootees that you had to tie around your shoes. So it was just kind of funny to see this bunch of vampires in these little boots.'

The scene sees Rathbone's Jasper attack Bella after she accidentally cuts her finger. To give the scene a visceral authenticity, Rathbone put so much intense effort into the part that Facinelli and Lutz struggled to hold him back during the scene.

Facinelli explained, 'He unleashed the madness; it was crazy. It took me and Kellan – non-acting – to hold him back.'

Lutz added, 'It's fun to work with your friends and see a side of them that you really don't expect. That's where the acting comes into play. Jackson did an amazing job portraying that scene, and it was fun being my character to try to stop him.' In fact, during one of the takes Rathbone accidentally knocked Elizabeth Reaser to the floor.

Greene's favourite scene, however, was when she and Stewart were in the Porsche making a mad dash to the airport to save Robert Pattinson's Edward Cullen in time. While the scene is intense on screen, in real life Greene and Stewart had a blast filming in the car. They would both spend most of the time in the car when the camera was off, singing and dancing.

She remembered, 'We started singing "Afternoon Delight" for some reason and just went off on crazy rants. We acted like we were twelve! So many people look at her like, "Oh, that Kristen girl, she's never smiling." But she's not this über-serious crazy person She's a cool girl who definitely giggles.

'It was really fun. I worked with a stuntman before actually driving it and learned how to do a bunch of unnecessary things that were fun, like fishtailing, and he was gonna teach me drifting. I drove it in a scene and came about two inches from the wall!'

And the fun would continue when they moved filming to Italy, with Greene and Michael Sheen having fun between takes spending their time looking at funny and bizarre clips on YouTube.

Of course, it wasn't all fun and laughs. Talking about the more serious aspects of *New Moon*, Stewart revealed, 'This is more… It's a severely emotional movie. Everybody knows that. That's the one big difference. This movie's not about discovery or falling in love. It's an intense emotion, but this is low. There are high points for her too. She's like a manic depressive basically.'

The love triangle ensured that the actors had 'to

go to some very dark places', according to Chris Weitz. '*Twilight* is about first love; *New Moon* is about heartache.'

Of Stewart, Weitz remarked, 'Kristen may be the most serious actor I've ever encountered. She took the job of portraying Bella's depression very seriously.'

Lutz noted about his co-star, 'She puts a lot of herself in that. She makes Bella not a weak character but a loner.'

Weitz added, 'There's every reason for a young actor to phone it in [not try as hard] on a franchise where the first movie has done incredibly well. But he [Pattinson] and Kristen take it really, really seriously and don't want to phone it in. They want to find some way to make these characters believable, credible to themselves and to the audience.'

The love triangle means that the fans have to plump for whom they want Bella to choose as her partner – Jacob or Edward. Facinelli unsurprisingly is in the latter camp.

'I gotta go Team Robert. He's my family. I love Taylor, but Rob plays my son so I got to keep it in the family.'

New Moon, New Feelings

'Nothing crossed the line while on the first film. I think it took a long time for Kristen to realise, OK, I've got to give this a go and really try to be with this person.' – Catherine Hardwicke

The success of *New Moon* ensured that the cast were never out of the headlines, with Greene moaning, 'My life is a crazy whirlwind right now. I'm just working and working and working.

'With the success of the film, there are a lot of things you get offered, places people want you to go just to have you there, and I really haven't been able to do that. Between this and other films, I've just been working. You know, I was a struggling actor, and I was modelling to pay bills. I was worried about rent, and I was living with two other people. To go from that to going, "I need a break, I need a day off" is a crazy thing.

'It's good, and it's tiring, but my mom being able to see what I'm doing every single day on the Internet? It's crazy! From nobody really knowing or really caring who you are or what you do to suddenly making headlines with what you're eating, where you're going, who you're hanging out and having coffee with is nuts. But I guess it helps when I'm walking into these rooms with directors and producers: all of a sudden they know who I am. That's the craziest thing.'

While Greene may have had struggles with the immediate impact of the *Twilight* series, she was not the only one.

The speculation of a romance between Stewart and Pattinson reached fever pitch just before *New Moon* was released. When the rumours started, she was still in a relationship with Michael Angarano, whom she had met on the 2004 TV movie *Speak*, when she was 13 and he 16. However, they began dating three years later. She has since split up with Angarano – which unsurprisingly fuelled the rumours of 'RPatz and KStew'.

Talks of clandestine dates organised with military-type precision were soon reported by the media. Seemingly, the pair would arrive and leave the venue separately to avoid suspicion and would check into secluded hotels under different names. The media would do everything they could to catch a glimpse of the pair together, with out-of-focus, snatched shots of them holding hands, peered at, scrutinised and analysed by the world's press.

Their romance is said to have been born out of a

friendship that evolved partly because of the intense and highly romantic situation they found themselves in through the filming of *Twilight* and *New Moon*. Their passion for the project was evident right from the start, with the pair spending nights at her home around the dining room table intently poring over the minute details of the script to get the dynamic between them just right. Not that they would have much trouble channelling it on screen.

Hardwicke told *Time* magazine, 'After I cast him, I told Rob, "Don't even think about having a romance with her. She's under 18. You will be arrested." I didn't have a camera in the hotel room. I cannot say. But in terms of what Kristen told me directly, it didn't happen on the first movie. Nothing crossed the line while on the first film. I think it took a long time for Kristen to realise, OK, I've got to give this a go and really try to be with this person.'

Ashley Greene noted, 'They're genuine, and they're very talented. It's like a secret potion that you can't really pinpoint, but they both have it.'

Peter Facinelli added, 'You look at these characters and want them to be together. And you want the actors to be together in real life.'

Talking to *Entertainment Weekly*, Stewart added, 'Maybe it's just my personality, but I'm never going to answer it. I probably would've answered it if people hadn't made such a big deal about it. I know that people are really funny about "Well, you chose to be an actor, why don't you just f**king give your whole life away? Can I have your firstborn child?"

'I've thought about this a lot. There's no answer that's not going to tip you one way or the other. I'm just trying to keep something. If people started asking me if I was dating Taylor, I'd be like "F**k off". I would answer the exact same way.'

Talking about the press attention, Pattinson remarked, 'It doesn't make any difference what you say. I've been across the country and it's like, "Oh, they were on secret dates!" It's like, "Where? I can't get out of my hotel room."'

Stewart admits, 'It's so retarded. We're characters in this comic book.'

The frenzy surrounding Pattinson has 'forced [him] into becoming a hermit'. He stayed in hotels – with his friend Tom Sturridge and his sister Lizzy keeping him company, with both of them sleeping on two foldout sofas. It has become his sanctuary – and it would have been a haven filled with more friends but they don't have enough money to come see him and he would 'feel like a dick paying their flights'. It's this sort of proof that shows that these levels of fame were never his intention.

'I'm trying not to drown,' he has said. 'I guess I'm not cut out to do a franchise. I'm not a crowd person.'

Pattinson's drama *Remember Me* would be released between *New Moon* and *Eclipse*. The film was the first movie he had worked on since the *Twilight* franchise began. During shooting, the mass fan attention got so bad that the film's production company hired security guards to take Pattinson from the set to the dressing room.

The media reported that on one occasion he was walking to his trailer with his security team when a large crowd of screaming girls started running towards him. What began like a scene from the classic Beatles movie *A Hard Day's Night*, where the band flee from girls though the streets, took a more scary turn when Robert ended up on the roads of Manhattan, where it was said he was struck by a taxi.

Of course what the media said and what actually happened were two different things. 'That was completely made up,' Pattinson explained. 'I was walking across the street, and there was one cab going about one mile an hour and it nudged my leg. The story ended up being how I got hit by a cab because of a mob of screaming fans, [but] it was four o clock in the morning and there was one person there – a paparazzo.'

Remember Me tells the story of a young man, Tyler, who is coping with the death of his brother. As he sleepwalks through life because of his bereavement, he ends up meeting a young woman, Ally (Emilie de Ravin), who seizes life to its fullest despite coping with the loss of someone close herself.

Talking about the script, which he didn't want to end after he had read it, Pattinson said, 'It's about a

23-year-old guy and knowing somebody for six weeks. You don't just fall in love and say "I'm in love" after six weeks. It's really a relationship story. It's very natural and the characters are incredibly real and well scripted.

'I have no qualms in saying that Jenny Lumet [the writer] is a genius.'

Like the one for *Twilight*, *Remember Me*'s audition scene showed huge chemistry between Pattinson and the actress he would be playing opposite – Ravin in this case.

She said, 'They'd been looking to cast my role for a while, looking at a lot of different girls. I read the script three weeks before they started shooting. I flew to New York to test with Rob and we immediately got along and had instant great chemistry, which is not an easy thing to come by. Obviously you're acting, but you want to have that connection with somebody. We had it. And I was thrown into a wardrobe fitting that same day.

'The relationship between Ally and Tyler is so beautifully developed. It's such an honest, organic, real love story. It's not your typical Hollywood love story. Neither one of them was really looking for it, but it just happened. Obviously there's a physical attraction, but also that thing you can't put into words. They're brought together in very random circumstances. It's not love at first sight, but they're intrigued at first sight. They've both had major family tragedies that, prior to their relationship, have closed them off, thinking no one can understand the way they really feel. They just get each other. There's no false performance. It's all open and who they are. That's sometimes beautiful and sometimes ugly and sometimes frustrating, but it's all on the table.'

Talking about the media attention Pattinson received, Ravin told MTV, 'There were a lot of crazy moments where you're filming on location and you're waiting for people to get out of the shot. People don't want to move. Rob and I would laugh about that. There was a scene where we're on a date at a carnival, and it was very exposed to media, paparazzi and fans. We were rehearsing, and you become so self-conscious of people watching you, and we both stopped and looked at each other and were like, "Wait, what are we doing?" You're taken out of your work mentality with hundreds of people watching you when you're just trying to figure out your scene.'

Ravin and Pattinson were briefly linked romantically. However, Ravin claims that they were just very good friends.

'It was so great being able to work with someone you immediately get along with and is incredibly talented and is driven to make the film as good as we can. Having someone you can go and talk with about a scene, and it's all very casual and easy, that made filming such a delight – having a friendship level and a commitment to the script. The way Rob and I developed our relationship onscreen was very natural, and just seeing what happened with scenes, what happens in the moment.'

Pierce Brosnan played Pattinson's father in the film, and remarked, 'I have no remaining ego whatsoever after shooting *Remember Me* with Robert last year. His trailer was down one end of the avenue, surrounded by girls, and mine was a very quiet little haven of solitude at the other end. Even when we were shooting in the heart of New York, I could actually hear when Rob left his trailer: the girls would be going so bonkers.'

The young cast of *Twilight* were highly in demand and their names have been linked with many big movie franchises. Pattinson was also briefly considered (and subsequently ruled out) as a replacement for Tobey Maguire in *Spider-Man*. And it wasn't just Pattinson: Kellan Lutz, too, was being favoured as the actor to play the named role in *Conan the Barbarian* – one made famous by Arnold Schwarzenegger in the 1982 movie and subsequent sequel two years later. However, another actor secured the part.

Ashley Greene, meanwhile, caused a stir when she stripped off for a saucy advertising campaign. With just body paint preserving her modesty, she appeared in a series of adverts for the soft drink SoBe.

She said of the campaign, 'It took the artist twelve hours to paint the SoBe scales on each skin suit, but it was totally worth it. It's an experience I'll never forget.

'We did two photoshoots, one on the beach and one in a secluded jungle-like setting, and it was incredible.'

And she credited her physical training for *Eclipse* – the third Meyer film – for perfecting her toned figure. 'We had a lot of action and fight training,' she said. 'So it really toned up my body for these pictures.'

Peter Facinelli juggled time between prepping for *Eclipse* and working on the critically acclaimed show *Nurse Jackie*, which is filmed in LA.

He said, 'I have had a very crazy schedule. There was a whole month where I was shooting *Eclipse* and *Nurse Jackie* at the same time. And I actually enjoyed it because I enjoy what I do.

'When I show up for work, it's very invigorating and I get energised by it. So there were times where I'd get off an airplane from a red-eye [an overnight flight] and have, like, three hours' sleep and then go straight to work. But, again, I'm having such a good time on the show... as soon as I get on the set, I have so much energy.'

'I mean, there were days where I was literally running for hours in the forest and then I jump on a plane and I would be on the *Nurse Jackie* set.'

He kept up to date with his fans using the social networking tool Twitter. 'It's a great way to share information with them and it's also a great way to entertain,' he said.

'I like being able to put a smile on people's faces and I like being able to also mix that up with sharing information with them that's important and also letting them know what I'm doing.'

However, he is quick to ensure that he doesn't abuse his dialogue with his fans, revealing, 'I mean I've had people come to me and say, "Hey, will you tweet this out?" There's like paid advertisement stuff. I'm not into that. I like to keep my Twitter pure. I don't want to sell my followers anything.'

In fact, in January 2010 he was the most tweeted celebrity on the Internet with more than 1.5 million followers.

Facinelli is also a regular at the annual Vampire Baseball events that spring up in American cites over the summer period – which see *Twilight* and *New Moon* stars pit their wits against other celebrity teams. Of course, fans hoping to see the Cullen clan play baseball will be disappointed that the actors can't achieve the same superhero antics as their screen counterparts.

When asked about Vampire Baseball just before an event in Portland in July 2009, Facinelli said, 'We're going to test our vampire baseball skills in front of a large crowd and I think a lot of people are going to find out that a lot of the cast members don't know how to throw a ball and they just made us look good.

'The Make-A-Wish Foundation asked if I would play and I thought it was for a really good cause. I like doing charity events because I think it's important to give back. I played baseball when I was younger but I haven't played in a long time, so it should be fun. I hope Rachelle's on my team. She's the one with the wicked curve ball, right?'

Robert Pattinson also showed his kind-hearted side by manning one of the donation lines for the Hope for Haiti telethon – which was held to raise money for victims of the huge earthquake that stuck the island in January 2010. He read out a story of a young Haitian girl who was trapped under the rubble.

Rob's willingness to use his celebrity to help out a good cause goes to show that he hasn't allowed the fame to go to his head, but has managed to remain grounded – and the same can be said for all the stars of *The Twilight Saga* films.

chapter thirteen

Eclipse

'I found that we've gotten to know each other better than you usually do on a movie set.' – Elizabeth Reaser

As Pattinson becomes more and more of a Hollywood success, he has suddenly found himself in the somewhat curious position whereby even his hair is looked at by studio bosses with huge interest.

So desperate were they to make sure their leading man looked perfect in every scene of *Eclipse*, the third in the *Twilight* series, that they had some bizarre concerns.

'The most ridiculous one on *Eclipse* is my hair. I swear I've never experienced anything like this. It's every single day.

'I'm doing fight scenes and there's a strand going down to my forehead and they're like, "We need to do it again because no one will recognise you! No one will know who it is!" I'm like, "Really, is my face that generic?" I have to look like the poster at all times. Just in case they want to use any clips for the trailer. Any clip at all! There were about five different people in different departments who, because of my forelock, ended up in tears!

'I've never felt so objectified in my life.'

It's not the first time that Pattinson has had problems with his hair on the *Twilight* franchise. During the early preparation work, Catherine Hardwicke wanted to experiment with longer hair to see what it would look like.

The hair stylist on the film, Mary Anne Valdes, said, 'If Catherine really liked the long hair, she would talk the studio into it. The hair extensions went on that day and we took them out the next. We agreed [that it should be short]. But Catherine had to see for herself that the short hair was best. If she hadn't seen the long hair, she'd still be wondering.'

Jackson Rathbone landed in hot water when his script for *Eclipse* – an early draft – managed to leak onto the Internet. Rathbone's name was emblazoned all over it.

It wasn't the first time that the franchise had had script troubles. There could have been trouble when a script for *New Moon* was found in a rubbish bin in Missouri shortly before filming began. Casey Ray, a passerby, found the script and another one called *Memoirs* in a litterbin. Luckily for the film's bosses, Ray showed her kind-hearted nature by giving it back to the studio rather than cashing in on her find.

As a darker aspect of the story, *Eclipse* sees the war between the vampires and werewolves escalate further, while the Edward–Bella–Jacob love triangle heats up.

Kristen Stewart said, 'I'm looking forward to seeing the love triangle actually becoming a problem. We sort of innocently touch on it in *New Moon* but it actually becomes something that is very, very real.'

Pattinson added, 'It's really funny how everyone looks at Edward as the hero, but he is continuously saved by the damsel in distress. I think he really realises that in *New Moon*. *Eclipse* is really him trying to catch up with Jacob because he's so out of the loop and he can't speak in superlatives any more. He's accepted being alive and he needs to catch up to Jacob.'

Once again, there would be a different person calling the shots for the new film – in this case the highly acclaimed director David Slade.

'At first, it's a little difficult," said Ashley Greene in an interview for *Vanity Fair*. "It's a lot of give and take. Everyone's different and has their own take on it, but it's been pretty good. You have to sit down and go, "This is what I've been doing, this is why I feel this way," and you have to take suggestions. Basically, it's about communication, and it hasn't been a problem yet.'

Reaser added, 'I like it. I think part of the fun of being an actor is getting to work with different directors and seeing their take on it, what they're passionate about. They all have different ideas about your character. David has a very interesting take on Esme. He's really passionate about her, that she's not just this nice, sweet gal, that she's still a vampire and she's still tearing up mountain lions in the middle of the night and drinking their blood. She's still the wild beast in a way. It's fun to think about that aspect of her character.'

'I've seen *Hard Candy*, and I think he did a great job on that,' Facinelli chipped in. 'And, I'm going to rent *30 Days of Night*. Once he was hired, I sent him an email saying that I'm excited to work with him, and he sent me back one saying, "Ditto."'

Flashbacks will also feature heavily in the film, with fans of the series getting to see the Cullen family before they turned into vampires. For *Eclipse* the actors underwent six weeks of fight training to show their action-packed side.

Greene told *Maxim* magazine, 'Yeah, I get to fight in *Eclipse*. My trainer is teaching me MMA [mixed martial arts] right now. So. Cool. But I feel if I were in a real fight, I'd get my ass kicked.'

Facinelli added, 'The Cullens get to roll up their sleeves and really get into the mix of things. The fight-scenes prep was tedious but fun. I enjoyed it immensely. Going to work and training, doing fight choreography and working out was fun. We had about five weeks to prep, so every day we were working really hard.

'It wasn't like digging ditches, but it was fun to be able to go in and be a part of that. It became very competitive within the cast.'

He added, 'What I like about the third movie is you

get to see a side of Carlisle you haven't seen before. You actually get to see what his vampire capabilities are because there are some great battle sequences. It's my favorite book. Carlisle is holding onto that humanity. He doesn't want to be a vampire.'

Kellan Lutz added, 'It's going to be one of those movies where guys who aren't fans of the *Twilight* series but like seeing a good kickass action movie are going to see it. And they're going to bring their girlfriends who are anti-*Twilight* because they don't want to be on that bandwagon.'

Bryce Dallas Howard is also making her debut in the franchise – replacing actress Rachelle LeFevre in the role of Victoria. (More details surrounding that drama can be found in the *Werewolves* book at the back of this one.) Howard's casting led to a wave of protest from *Twilight* fans, shocked at seeing one of their favourite cast members being axed because of a scheduling oversight (LeFevre's work on a low-budget movie overran into *Eclipse*'s shooting schedule).

However, Howard was quick to get in the fans' good books by leaping to the rescue of Robert Pattinson – who has been hampered with rumours that he suffers from poor hygiene.

It all started when an 'industry insider' told the waiting media, 'He stinks. I mean, it's awful. He never showers, and it drives people on the set crazy. He completely reeks.'

However, Howard was quick to quash the rumours

– revealing that he brushed his teeth so much that he damaged one of them.

She told *New York* magazine, 'Actually, he's incredibly hygienic. He told me this story that made me crack up. He was like, "Oh, I have to go to the dentist." And I was like, "Oh no, what happened? Just a check-up?" And he was like, "No, I chipped a tooth." And I was like, "How?" And he was like, "Flossing." Who does that? I don't even floss. So he's hygienic. Trust me.'

Talking more about Robert, she added, 'He's such a sweet young man, and there's such a distinctive difference between him and Edward Cullen. He does such a wonderful job embodying that character, and bringing that character to life. But when you meet him, he's such a down-to-earth, humble person, you feel bad freaking out around him.'

Howard's inclusion pleased Jackson Rathbone, however, with the young actor admitting in interviews long before she was cast that she was his celebrity crush.

As it had been with *New Moon*, the set of *Eclipse* was like returning home to family for the actors who play the Cullen clan. Elizabeth Reaser told *Vanity Fair*, 'I found that we've gotten to know each other better than you usually do on a movie set. It's hard to stay in touch with people, and over the years you kind of move on. This week, we've come back and it feels more like a family than friends. In terms of how we interact, we're shooting on this set that is an exact replica of the house that we shot in Portland originally. It's funny, I've been having all of these memories of little moments from two years ago – it feels very much the same.'

Eclipse promises to be the best film of the series so far – not that the actors are resting on their laurels. They have plenty of other films coming up that will showcase their talents.

chapter fourteen

What Next for the Cullens?

'People have become very passionate about – about my character, but also about me, really relating to me and wanting to be my best friend.'
– Ashley Greene

The *Twilight* series is a springboard for the careers of the actors who play the Cullen clan.

Of course, before they start focusing on other projects, there is the small matter of the very last book in the *Twilight* saga, *Breaking Dawn*.

Ashley Greene said of *Breaking Dawn* during promotion of the first *Twilight* book, 'I'm getting through it. It's a big book! I like it but it's definitely just a different twist and it's not so heavy on the romance like the past three were, but I still like it. I really like the writing style.'

Facinelli, however, hopes that the filmmakers don't show more of the adult content in the book, since he might not be able to take his young daughters to the cinema to see the film.

'I have a twelve-year-old daughter. She's a fan, and I'd want her not to feel left out or awkward. Hopefully, it's a PG-13 type of situation. I'm sure the producers and directors know what they want – and especially what they are doing – but I'm sure they don't want to alienate fans.'

Despite, initial difficulties in dealing with the media attention, *Twilight* opened so many doors for Greene, and for that she's incredibly grateful.

She added, 'But with this film in particular, people have become very passionate about – about my character, but also about me, really relating to me and wanting to be my best friend. And so they cry, and they get so nervous. You kind of don't know what to do. I give them a hug or whatever. People ask if I get annoyed, but you can't really get annoyed at something like that.

'But, you know, most of my fans are really respectful and great. It's too early for me to be jaded. Ask me in ten years or something… I just booked a lead in a film, and probably part of it was because they know that there are all these fans. I mean, hopefully it's because of my talent, too.'

The film she was talking about was *The Apparition*. The supernatural chiller sees Ashley and *Gossip Girl* actor Sebastian Stan play a couple who discover a ghost in their house.

'The great thing about this film is that it's really serious. It's more of a thriller. And, for once, I got cast first. They consulted me on the lead male, and we're talking back and forth about this character, so it's sort of a new stepping stone in my career.

'I relish it. Part of it might be that I did get to work so closely with these people, and see close up how they handle things. But I'm really excited. One of the coolest feelings was when I was reading with people for a part, and this guy came in, and I was just like, "That's the guy."'

She will also star in *Skateland* – a coming-of-age drama set in a Texas skating rink in the 1980s. She will team up with her fellow Cullen family member Kellan Lutz in the film *Warrior*. They may play brother and sister in the *Twilight* series, but this time she will be Lutz's girlfriend in the film, which tells the tale of a Lacrosse player (Lutz played the same sport in *90210*) who lashes out at life after his father is killed. However, his dad's old Marine buddy comes into his life in order to straighten him out.

Lutz said of the part, '[He] has to cope with not having a father. So he just goes on a rebellious stage. He goes away to this camp and really matures, and becomes a man. Then he comes back and he finishes up and ties up all his loose ends. It's a really good story. It's really well written.'

Greene added, 'I'm the coach's daughter. He plays lacrosse, and basically the story is that his dad is a Marine, so they move around and they end up moving him back to his dad's hometown, where he played lacrosse.

'[It] is about Kellan's journey. It's very much Kellan's movie, which is really exciting for him. It's his journey that he goes through, with trials and errors, and his temper and stuff like that. And I join forces with him, and my dad doesn't like that very much, so we deal with that. It's going to be cute.'

Before *Warrior*, the pair were due to work together on an independent drug drama called *Strife*, but they both left the project.

'We were in talks for doing *Strife*, but that happened way before *Twilight*, and it just never came through,' said Greene. 'But there's something cool where me and Kellan get the opportunity to work together a lot. I love him to death.'

He has also signed on to play Mandy Moore's character's husband in a new romantic comedy entitled *Love, Wedding, Marriage*, which tells the story of a woman (Moore) whose attempts to get her recently separated parents back together puts her own marriage in jeopardy. *Saving Private Ryan* actor Dermot Mulroney will direct the picture.

But Kellan Lutz also has his eyes set on an already existing franchise: '[I'm] focused on becoming that new action hero. I want to be Jason Bourne… and take over that franchise. I love doing stunts and shooting guns and doing fight scenes.'

As for Pattinson, he stars in the period epic *Unbound Captives*. The film, which was written by actress Madeline Stowe, has been in the works for a long time. Hollywood has been desperate for years to put on the big screen the story of a young woman who seeks help from a frontiersman after her children are kidnapped by the Comanche tribe, but Stowe refused to sell it to the studios unless she played the lead role.

However, she finally decided to make it after she signed on to direct the film instead. Rachel Weisz will now play the female part, with Robert Pattinson teaming up along with Hugh Jackman. It will mark Stowe's directorial debut.

Speaking about the part, Pattinson said, 'I can't say much about that, but I know the script needs me to learn Comanche. Maybe it'll be like *Dances with Wolves* with my part entirely in Comanche.'

While little is known at the moment about Pattinson's character, he has been described as a fierce, silent and standoffish warrior. The role is expected to see Pattinson flex his action muscles by getting into fights and riding horses bareback.

He has also signed on to star in 2011's *Bel Ami*, which is based on the 1885 short story. It sounds as if we'll see Robert in a completely different light in this one. He plays a 'totally amoral' social climber, who manipulates a series of powerful and wealthy women to get what he wants.

A script leaked to US magazine *Life & Style* reports that Pattinson enjoys saucy screen romps with a number of actresses such as Christina Ricci, Uma

Thurman and Kristin Scott Thomas. The magazine describes Pattinson's love scene with Scott Thomas as 'rough and ravenous'.

Pattinson himself describes his character as an 'animal' and someone who 'just rips off and screws over all of his friends'.

He has also signed on to star in *Water for Elephants*, a drama set in the Depression era. Pattinson will play a college student studying veterinary medicine who decides instead to join up with a circus, looking after the animals, following his heartbreak over his parents' death.

The film will see him team up with his Reese Witherspoon, his old *Vanity Fair* co-star. She will play one of the circus performers. Because of the huge media attention and the success of the *Twilight* movies, Pattinson came seventh in *Forbes* magazine's Fastest Rising Stars List.

He has also started to take things less seriously, and is learning to trust others with his career choices. 'When I was seventeen until I was twenty, I had this massive, baseless confidence, this very clear idea of myself and how I would achieve success, which involved making decisions.

'I saw myself picking up the phone and saying, "Absolutely not" or, "Definitely yes" – having control. Except you have to figure out whether the way you think at nineteen or twenty has any value.

'And eventually I understood, with all that control,

which was probably illusory, I wasn't progressing. Seriously, you eventually realise you can't make every single decision.'

While the future looks great for Pattinson and the rest of the Cullen clan, He's still not sure if acting is the profession he'll enjoy for the rest of his life.

'I'm not massively concerned about doing lots of acting. If it all just went right now I'd be like, "All right, I don't really care." That's probably a stupid thing to say, but I don't, really. I think it'd be much worse to do a load of stuff that's really bad. Because then you can't go into another career. If you've made an idiot out of yourself, you're never going to be taken seriously, as a lawyer or something, if you're, like, a joke actor. The only thing I want from anything is to not be embarrassed.'

One thing for sure is that Pattinson is not chasing another huge franchise any time soon. 'There's no point,' he told *Vanity Fair*. 'I mean, I don't have any material desires at all. I wear the same clothes every single day. I don't buy anything. And I don't go out anymore, either!'

As for the Juilliard-trained Elizabeth Reaser, she has no idea what her career is going to throw up next.

'My career's been a steady, interesting, weird, frustrating, fun journey at all different times. I've never really had that one thing where suddenly my whole life has changed. It's been very steady.

'I've been looking for a play for a while. The last play I did was at Williamstown; it was a play called *Top Girls* by Caryl Churchill. I was physically ill every night from being so nervous, but I'm looking to do [another play].'

For Kellan Lutz, the role of Emmett Cullen has been a dream one. 'We're all crossing our fingers, and we all want to finish the series. And we want Stephenie to write more books if she could.'

Nikki Reed has two lead roles to look forward to seeing herself in on the big screen: in the horror film *Chain Letter* (2010) and the psychological high-school drama *Privileged* (2010). Oddly enough, *Chain Letter* was shot before she worked on *Twilight* – and it came at a time when she was seriously thinking about quitting acting.

She said in 2008, 'I'm always categorised as the "indie girl" and to do that movie, for me, I suppose it was challenging in a way. I change my mind about whether or not I want to be an actor all the time.

'Right before *Chain Letter*, I had moved to Hawaii to go back to school because I decided I was never going to be an actor again. Then I got *Chain Letter*, and I thought, "You know what? What a fun way to walk out of this business." To do a fun horror movie. I actually thought that. Like, OK, this is something I haven't done. You know, I got some other things and some other offers while I was up there and I was, like, "I just don't want to hear it. I don't want to play the bad girl any more. I don't want to play the seductress. I just want to go to school ..." And then this came along.'

Jackson Rathbone is determined to flirt with both mainstream and independent film success. Proving this, one film he starred in was *Girlfriend* (2010), an intense, low-budget drama involving a love triangle between two ex-high-school sweethearts (Rathbone and Shannon Woodward) and a Down's-syndrome twentysomething named Evan.

Woodward explains, 'Jackson's character and I have an actual relationship that has since gone sour that still exists, but my relationship with Evan is a friendship. And he doesn't quite understand what having a girlfriend means.'

The director of *Girlfriend*, Justin Lerner, explained to MTV how he came up with the inspiration for the movie: 'We're in an economic crisis, and [the film is set] in a small town where there's lots of lying, deceit, jealousy, rage, violence. Evan is pure good. He's pure innocent love. How fascinating would it be to put pure, innocent, unconditional love into this world, and see what happens.' 100 Monkeys provide the music to the film.

Rathbone is also starring in *The Last Airbender*, which is directed by *Sixth Sense*'s M Night Shyamalan. It's based on the popular Nickelodeon kids' show, and Rathbone plays Sokka, a young warrior of the Southern Water tribe.

'It's a fantastic show. I've always loved that kind of deep, mythical fantasy. It's got a lot about the four elements: water, fire, earth, wind. It's just really cool. It's a really interesting series and such a cool character. I've always liked the show, and I thought it would be fun.

'For me, it's a great chance to show my range a little bit more. It's a chance to do something a little funnier. Something less serious than Jasper.

'It's just an action-packed, epic film. I'm starting to do martial-arts training, which is going to be so much fun, and we're doing a lot of interesting work with the green screen [against which action is performed for post-production computer-generated imagery to be added]. It's such a mythical world. We get to go to Asia, go film abroad. It's just going to be such a blast.'

While an adaptation of a children's animated show might be seen a strange project for a director used to making more grown-up films, Rathbone disagrees.

'I think *Airbender* has a lot of suspenseful twists as a TV show, but I think it's something he's really looking forward to, for expanding his own horizons. He has kids. How many films has he made that his kids would be able to watch? So I think it's really great that he's making a family film. I have a sister; it's exciting to make a film that my whole family can enjoy.'

The film was hit by controversy over its decision to

cast white actors such as Rathbone and several others in roles that were Asian characters in the TV show.

The young actor was quick to explain, however, telling MTV, 'I think it's one of those things where I pull my hair up, shave the sides, and I definitely need a tan. It's one of those things where, hopefully, the audience will suspend disbelief a little bit.'

Facinelli, however, is just desperate to work with his wife Jennie Garth on a TV show. She told *E! Online*, 'My husband is writing a script we're developing for television.' Garth has since left *90210*, citing wanting to spend more time with her family and to write a children's book as the reasons.

Facinelli said, 'I try to do things that I haven't done before; hopefully I'll continue to do so, and continue to surprise the audience and surprise myself.'

Whether it's further success on the big screen, small screen or stage, it's clear that the future is bright for the *Twilight* actors.

Facinelli added, 'We're pretty much a family on and off set. After work we enjoy each other's company. We go out to dinners. We had this experience together. There were no egos involved when we started *Twilight*, and there are still no egos involved, and that's so nice to see that people's heads haven't grown. They're still the same people who started the journey.'

Proof that perhaps, while the *Twilight* films will end, the Cullen family, like all families, will stick together.

werewolves

v

vampires

THE WEREWOLVES

MARTIN HOWDEN

JB

JOHN BLAKE

Published by John Blake Publishing Ltd,
3 Bramber Court, 2 Bramber Road,
London W14 9PB, England

www.johnblakepublishing.co.uk

First published in paperback in 2010

ISBN: 978 1 84454 961 0

British Library Cataloguing-in-Publication Data:

A catalogue record for this book is available from the British Library.

Design by www.envydesign.co.uk

Printed in Great Britain by CPI Bookmarque, Croydon, CR0 4TD

1 3 5 7 9 10 8 6 4 2

Front cover images and internal photographs reproduced with kind
permission of Rex Features.

Papers used by John Blake Publishing are natural, recyclable products made
from wood grown in sustainable forests. The manufacturing processes conform to
the environmental regulations of the country of origin.

Every attempt has been made to contact the relevant copyright-holders,
but some were unobtainable. We would be grateful if the appropriate
people could contact us.

Contents

Introduction

Choosing the werewolf section of the book, means you're howling mad for Jacob Black and his Wolf Pack.

Jacob Black is a member of the Native American Quileute tribe, and the son of Billy Black, an old family friend of Charlie Swan, Bella's father. When Charlie's daughter returns to the small town of Forks, Washington State, Jacob is instantly smitten. While Bella treats him as just a friend, preferring to spend her time obsessing over the vampire Edward Cullen, she ends up becoming increasingly close to him, following a split from Edward. Not only does she discover that her Edward was a vampire, but that Jacob, too, possesses some supernatural abilities of his own.

He was becoming a werewolf – although the

Quileute tribal wolves are in fact different from 'true werewolves' who transform on a full moon. They are shape-shifting humans who change into wolves whenever they wish, and you can see more of them in the eagerly awaited blockbuster *Eclipse*, the third film in the series.

Sam Uley is the leader of the Wolf Pack, and which also includes Quil Ateara, Embry Call, Paul and Jared.

But what do you know about the actors who play them? Read on to discover more about *Twilight*'s famous wolves.

chapter one

Taylor's Beginnings

'It was a very, very hard decision. Our family and friends did not want us to go. But our choices were: we could stay in Michigan and I could give up acting…or we could move to California and I could continue to act.' – Taylor Lautner

Taylor Daniel Lautner was born on 11 February 1992 to Deborah and Daniel, a software manager and airline pilot respectively.

While it would be a long time before their son would land the role of Jacob Black in the *Twilight* series, Lautner seemed destined even as a child to play a werewolf – he was once caught attempting to bite the other kids at day care.

Born in Michigan's Grand Rapids, he lived in a little house on Rosewood Avenue. Because both his parents' relatives lived nearby, Lautner was never short of affection. And the young boy was never slow to flash his cute smile to charming effect.

Talking about his hometown to *Grand Rapids Press*, he explained, 'I love coming back here. In LA,

1

whatever you do for fun, you gotta spend money. Here, you go jet skiing on a lake. It's such a fun place for me. I go fishing with one set of grandparents, I go quad riding with the other set.

'We go trap shooting. It's so much fun. Here, people are way more down to earth.'

When he was six, Taylor became a big brother to Makena. Just as Taylor was spoilt for affection, so was Makena. Taylor was about as good a big brother as a baby sister could want.

'My sister and I would always be spies when I was younger. We'd be in the house, and I'd hide something, and I'd act like we were secret agents and spies. And I'd tell her that it was really happening, and she still believes me to this day,' he revealed.

By the time Makena was born, the family had moved to a bigger home. And the reason they moved was because the family had a terrifyingly lucky escape.

Taylor was four at the time. His dad was away once more on a flight. His mother decided the two should go and visit one of his aunts and stay the night there. That very night, their house burnt down.

Taylor looks back at the incident now and reflects on just how lucky he was. 'The police called and told us our house had burned down. If my aunt hadn't invited us to sleep over…Well, wow!'

It seems that the near escape made him want to live his life to the full, as Taylor seems to soak up hobbies and interests like a sponge.

2

He was obsessed with sport at a young age, and the sight of a young Taylor wrestling with his friends in and out of the house, no matter what the weather, was to be a regular one. If he wasn't wrestling, then he would be playing a number of other sports that took his interest, including swimming, baseball, soccer, horse riding and basketball.

It wasn't just sport that the young Taylor took a fancy to: he was also fascinated with acting, and soon dreamt of becoming an actor. But, when Taylor was six, he discovered something else that would take over his young life. He enrolled at nearby Fabiano's Karate & Fitness Center, and he took to marital arts incredibly well.

The karate school owner, Tom Fabiano, remembered Taylor as a willing, hardworking and talented pupil.

'A friend of mine through my mom's work had his sons in karate and my parents took me to check out the class. I liked it and began karate when I was six. I really liked class because of all the games we got to play, like Swords and Spears, Sensei Says, et cetera. I didn't really care too much for the push-ups and all the hard work. I really started because of the fun games,' he told Karateangels.com.

It quickly became clear to Fabiano that Taylor was a natural, winning local contests with ease. At seven years old he shocked everyone when he competed in the nationals and won three trophies.

With martial arts taking up much of his young life, it looked as if his interest in acting was going to take a backseat. However, in a bizarre twist of fate, while he was competing at the national championships, he met a new instructor who would not only teach him a new form of martial arts that he had invented but also give him the guidance needed to break into the movie business.

The karate instructor was Mike Chat, the Blue Power Ranger in the hugely popular kids 1990s TV show and film, *Mighty Morphin Power Rangers*. Chat was impressed with what he saw of Taylor and invited him to his XMA Camp in Los Angeles. XMA was a new form of marital arts invented by Chat, himself a seven-times world karate champion, and combines styles of dance, yoga, tae kwon do and kickboxing to fun and entertaining effect.

For someone who was a fan of Chat's show, it didn't take long for Taylor to say yes to being taught by one of his screen heroes. For Taylor, who had only been taught traditional martial-arts style, this was a huge chance – and it was something he immediately grasped.

'I fell in love. I was doing aerial cartwheels with no hands. My favourite martial artist is Mike Chat. He's helped me so much.'

Asked about the difference between Xtreme martial arts and regular martial arts, Taylor explained, 'Regular martial arts is traditional, with no music and no flips choreographed into it. But Xtreme martial arts is choreographed to music. It's very fast-beat uptempo and you put a lot of acrobatic manoeuvres into the routine.

'[My favourite move is] called a corkscrew. It's a back flip off one leg and then you do a 360 in the air and I land it in the splits. I was the first competitor to ever land that in the national karate circuit.'

Taylor decided to keep up both his traditional karate classes and Xtreme Martial Arts lessons with Chat. The former saw him landing a black belt at eight, while the latter was a little bit more difficult. With Chat's classes taking place in LA and with Taylor's dad often away because of his pilot job, it proved a difficult constant commute from Michigan to LA.

Taylor's parents and Chat worked out a training schedule that would see him flying to LA as often as he could – sometimes even taking an overnight flight back from LA to make sure he didn't miss out on an important test.

They did this for a year and it became obvious to everyone involved that Lautner was something of a star. At eight he won three gold medals and became the Junior World Forms and Weapons Champion at the World Karate Association Championship, followed by the Warrior Trophy Cup for the 17-and-under age group at a World Karate Association, aged 9.

Eventually the commuting began to take its toll and Taylor was exhausted. He decided to take a year off from competing in karate tournaments. He would still train but, after three years of intense practice, he needed a break.

The break also meant that he could go back to

enjoying playing other sports such as American football, and spending more time with his friends.

But he did miss the lure of competing in martial-arts tournaments, and in 2003 he rejoined the circuit, winning World Junior Weapons Championship and finding himself ranked number one in the world at the North American Sport Karate Association's Black Belt Open Forms, Musical Weapons, Traditional Weapons and Traditional Forms.

Chat was not only hugely impressed with Lautner's martial-arts ability when he first met him, he saw that the young, charismatic kid could have a future in Hollywood, too, and he quickly set about getting Lautner, who was now desperate to get into acting, some work.

Taylor told *Reel Answers*, 'The first audition that my karate instructor sent me out on was a Burger King commercial. It was kind of like a karate audition in that they were basically looking for martial arts stuff. And they were looking for someone older, but he wanted to send me anyway to get the experience.

'So, I met with the casting director, we talked, and she asked for some poses. It was funny, though, because at the time, I didn't even know what a pose was [laughing]! I was only seven. But I learned quickly and did some poses for them. And I really liked it. I thought it went well, but I didn't get it.'

Despite not getting the part, it was clear that he was well and truly bitten by the acting bug. So he was no doubt overjoyed when Chat asked him if he wanted to go to California for a month to try to land some movie and TV roles.

A chance to be near Hollywood was too good an opportunity for him to turn down, but he still had second thoughts.

Talking to *Teen Vogue*, he said, 'At first, I wasn't interested, but he said I could stay at his house for a few weeks, meet with some agents, go on auditions. By the end of that month I liked it. Taking on roles that were the opposite of what I could be in real life? That's still my favourite thing.'

Indeed, as soon as he agreed to give acting a try, he got several auditions. It was a great vindication that he had made the right choice – especially as he booked his first role so soon after testing the waters in Hollywood.

In 2001, he starred in the martial-arts action film *Shadow Fury*. It wasn't a big part but it was one that saw him fight on screen just like his hero Jean-Claude Van Damme.

Buoyed by the success of that, he was soon receiving offers to come and read for parts from casting agents all over LA. But Lautner found himself once again constantly commuting from his hometown to Hollywood.

It was a crazy schedule, and one that couldn't last much longer. In the back of his mind, Lautner knew there would be very tough decisions to be made.

Knowing there was no chance that they could keep

commuting every time he got an audition, he would have to persuade his parents to move to Hollywood. They decided to head to LA for a month, to see if it was worth making the move permanent. Despite attending several auditions, he didn't book one part. It seemed his chance to conquer Hollywood was already coming to an end.

But, on the day that they were to head back to Michigan, he received a callback for a role. He wasn't successful in actually getting the part, but it proved to his parents that he'd obviously made an impression to be at least considered. It was then that Lautner's family decided to move for good.

As Taylor concedes, it was a difficult choice: 'It was a very, very hard decision. Our family and friends did not want us to go. But our choices were: we could stay in Michigan and I could give up acting – I would have had to because it would have been crazy to continually fly out from Michigan to California each time there was an audition – or we could move to California and I could continue to act. I told my parents I didn't want to give up acting. And, after weighing the good with bad, they agreed to move.'

And it was a decision they would not regret.

chapter two
Taylor the Actor

'It's no surprise to me that he was going to go on to great things.'
– Robert Rodriguez

Taylor Lautner enrolled in Valencia High School in Santa Clarita, CA, where he stayed before graduating early because of his film success. Despite his combat skills, Lautner insists that he never used it in school, preferring to keep away from any of the more unruly classmates.

'Nobody's ever wanted to start a fight. I stay away from all that stuff. It's never really happened.'

After the family had made their move to LA permanent, roles in *Summerland*, *The Bernie Mac Show* and *My Wife and Kids* followed for the young Lautner, and the last of these gave him a chance to act a completely different persona.

'I got to be a bully and push this little kid around! That was fun because I'm normally not a bully

9

because my parents wouldn't allow me to do that. I'm just not that person, but it was fun to experience something new.'

But it was to be in 2005, when he was 13, that he would begin to enjoy some regular work, bagging a recurring role as the voice of Youngblood in the cartoon *Danny Phantom*. It was a role that he had immense fun with.

Voice work has proven to be a lucrative career plan for Lautner. Not only did he work on the aforementioned *Danny Phantom*, there were also roles in *What's New, Scooby-Doo?*, *The Adventures of Silas and Brittany* and *He's a Bully, Charlie Brown*.

'My favourite one so far was probably Youngblood on *Danny Phantom*. I've done three episodes so far and he's a lot of fun to voice. Probably because I'm a kid-bully-pirate. I'm an evil ghost and a pirate and get to say stuff like "Arrrgh!"'

But it was live action that Lautner wanted to make an impact with, and he got his wish after he landed a major role in *Spy Kids* director Robert Rodriquez's family film *The Adventures of Sharkboy and Lavagirl*.

During the audition, Rodriquez asked the young Lautner to show some superhero poses. It was a question that he was more than ready for, and he shocked the director with some flashy martial-arts moves. Not only did he impress Rodriquez, but, more importantly, he also impressed the director's son Racer, who came up with the idea for the film.

But Taylor couldn't celebrate getting the part just yet. 'Unfortunately, LA was just the first spot that they stopped at before auditioning throughout the rest of the country. But, fortunately, thousands of auditions later, they came back to me and told me I'd got the part.'

Rodriquez said, 'He was the first actor we saw for *Sharkboy and Lavagirl* and we picked him right off.

'We knew he was the guy. He had so much personality. It's no surprise to me that he was going to go on to great things. He kind of made himself. In fact, he may have walked in fully formed.'

Taylor played Sharkboy, one half of a superhero team dreamt up by a 10-year-old boy who is constantly getting bullied at school. However, Max – the bullied boy – gets a shock when the figments of his imagination turn out to not only be real but to also need his help.

When he found out he'd got the role, Taylor enjoyed a huge party thrown by his parents.

'We went out to dinner to celebrate, we went out with friends and I had a surprise at a restaurant with some friends. And we were all very excited when we found out. We couldn't sleep,' remembered Taylor.

It was a dream role for Taylor because he got to spend his day doing what he loves the most: acting and doing action scenes. And, when Rodriquez found out the full extent of Lautner's martial-arts abilities, he asked him to choreograph the fight scenes in the film.

It may have been his biggest acting role to date, but there were no nerves for Taylor. He certainly made an impression on the set of the film. The young actor was a constant whirlwind of energy on set, alongside his two young co-stars Taylor Dooley (Lavagirl) and Cayden Boyd (Max).

'We had a lot of fun on the set. After we were done shooting, the three of us would go behind the set and play hide 'n' seek and climb trees…And we all see each other a lot since we live only a few blocks from one another. We go out to dinner together and we have many of our friends from the set over for sleepovers.'

As proof that it's a small world, Dooley just so happened to also hail from Michigan, and in fact, she and Lautner only lived a few blocks apart there.

And the pair would remain close afterwards, often making home movies together, because not only did Taylor Lautner want to star in films, he wanted to direct as well after enjoying every minute of the experience of working with Robert Rodriguez.

While promoting the film, he revealed, 'I would love to go the acting route, but, if I couldn't, I would want to be like Robert Rodriguez, a writer and director, because I do a lot of home movies with Taylor Dooley and her younger brother. We make a lot of films together and we're actually in the middle of one right now. So we have a lot of fun doing that. And I'd really love to do that if the acting thing didn't work out.'

Rodriquez made sure the atmosphere was an

enjoyable one for the young cast, to ensure they didn't get bored waiting for each shot to be set up.

'Everybody loved working with him,' added Lautner. 'He played video games with us on the set. For instance, while I'd be shooting a particular scene, he'd be off playing video games with Taylor [Dooley]. It was so much fun.'

It wasn't all fun and games however. Because he was so young, Lautner still had to go to school – in this case in the form of an on-set tutor. Not surprisingly, that didn't go down too well with Lautner. 'My least favourite part was the three hours of school on the set every day. School is good, but it's not really fun. If it had to be anything, it would have to be that!'

The Adventures of Sharkboy and Lavagirl wasn't well received, with the BBC calling it a 'ceaselessly inventive but ultimately tedious caper set in a three-dimensional CG world', before going on to say, 'Unfortunately, there's no rhyme or reason to the delirious imagery put before us. Nor are the leads surrounded by the kind of stellar ensemble that made the *Spy Kids* films as enjoyable for adults as they were for kids. *Sharkboy* works fine as a Ritalin substitute for kids with ADHD [attention-deficit hyperactivity disorder]. Their mums and dads, though, will be reaching for the paracetamol.'

Ouch!

Despite the reviews, working on the movie gave Taylor newfound confidence that he was good enough to make a career out of acting – and he quickly found himself starring alongside Steve Martin in his next movie. He played Elliot, the son of the Bakers' rivals, in *Cheaper by the Dozen 2*.

Talking about his role in the film, Lautner noted, 'It's about the disorganised family, Steve Martin's family. And they have competitions with this new family that they meet on summer vacation.

'My mom is Carmen Electra and my dad is Eugene Levy. We're this straight-A, athletic, organised family. And we just have all these competitions like canoeing and jet skiing.'

Taylor loves working on films because not only does he get better and better at acting with each role that he does, but he also makes new friends.

'My favourite part of being in a movie is that you get to meet a lot of nice people and you get good relationships from that, and it's a lot of fun to meet those new people. And it's fun playing characters not like yourself and being someone totally different for about three months.'

It also gave him a chance to work alongside a genuine comedy legend in Steve Martin. 'It was an awesome opportunity to work with Steve. He was always nice to the kids, making sure he talked to everyone. Besides being nice, he is also an excellent role model on being prepared and working hard.'

Taylor was now a bona fide movie star, and he was starting to reap the benefits.

'Ten-year-old boys were the ones who first recognised me,' recalled Taylor. 'I'd be in the store, and boys would whisper to their moms. Then the moms would say, "Excuse me, are you Sharkboy?" I just thought it was so cool. I couldn't believe people wanted my picture.

'All my fans have been really supportive and encouraging. It means a lot to me when parents have said to me that they appreciate the role model they feel I am to their kids. I love little kids and when parents feel good about who they look up to, that makes me feel good inside.'

But, if he thought he was famous then, wait till he saw his next role!

chapter three

Taylor's Big Break

'The fans would love anybody who played Jacob. I'm just lucky to be the one who got the chance.' – Taylor Lautner

It seems that some of the greatest horror characters on the printed page have been the result of a particularly fevered dream. Mary Shelley awoke with an image burned into her brain that would later become the creature in *Frankenstein*; and Robert Louis Stevenson's childhood night terrors remained with him till adulthood, when he would use the dream-generated fear as the inspiration for the book *Dr Jekyll and Mr Hyde*.

Like the products of those two authors, *Twilight* came to Stephenie Meyer in a dream.

'I had a dream about a vampire and a woman talking in a meadow. It came from nowhere. Once I started I didn't need another dream. The story wrote itself,' said Meyer.

She added, 'June 2, 2003, I know the exact day that

I woke up from the dream and started writing. I got the idea from a dream. It sounds cheesy but it was a great dream. The meadow scene in the movie [*Twilight*] is basically the dream that I had when I woke up. I wanted to know what happened to those characters.

'I was so afraid that I would forget this great dream that I wrote ten pages, pretty much the whole of Chapter 13, and then after that I just wanted to know what happened. I didn't expect to write a novel – just a chance to play with the characters in my head. When I finished it no one was more shocked than me to see I had finished a book.'

She went on to say that Chapter 13 of the book is 'essentially a transcript of my dream'. In fact, Meyer claimed she doesn't see herself writing stories but transcribing them from her head. She added, 'I had always told myself stories my whole life and assumed that everyone does. You know, it's funny: in *Jane Eyre*, which is something I've read forty million times, there's this scene where she shows Rochester her paintings. And she explains that in her head it was so different. And Rochester replies that she captured just a wisp of what she was seeing. I used to paint, and I won a few watercolour contests, but I could never get it to look exactly like it did in my head. But, with writing, I discovered I could get it to look exactly like it did in my head.'

Twilight is told from the perspective of Bella, a 17-year-old girl who is forced to move from her mother's home of sunny Scottsdale to her father's rain-drenched world in the small town of Forks. After enrolling in the local school and making a small group of friends, she is intrigued by the Cullen clan, a group of impossibly attractive boys and girls. Then Edward appears.

Constantly described as the most beautiful person ever, he embarks with Bella on a passionate, dramatic and dangerous romance. If Meyer's original draft had been published, however, the series might have gone a whole different way. In the first draft, Bella and Edward get married at the end.

The result of Stephenie's dream went on to become a massive success, spawning three other books in the series – *New Moon*, *Eclipse* and *Breaking Dawn*. The four books have sold more than 70 million copies worldwide.

Born in Connecticut on Christmas Eve 1974, Meyer ended up being the bookworm among six siblings. Raised as a Mormon, she buried her head in the many books that were available in her household, while her two sisters and three brothers made use of the huge space outside, building huts and later a paintball range.

Talking about the outskirts of Phoenix, where they ended up settling, she told *Vanity Fair*, 'It was a free-for-all land. Later, my brothers made it a lot more weaponized!'

She has both her mother and her father to thank for giving her the inspiration to write *Twilight*. From her mother's side she became fascinated by love stories: 'She was the one that had the Austen in the house. The reason I'm obsessed with the love side of any story is my mom. I always evaluate a story on relationships and the characters.'

Her dad, meanwhile, nourished her interest with nightly tales of fantastic, faraway adventures in another world. She would become so frustrated when he finished telling the stories at night that she would steal the book and hide in the closet the next morning trying to find out what happened next.

'I felt like I was doing something wrong, like I wasn't supposed to sneak ahead.'

It was senior vice-president of the publishers Little, Brown and Company, Megan Tingley, who first saw the potential of the books. She was handed the manuscript just before she had to embark on plane journey for work. To say she wasn't expecting an enjoyable read was an understatement. For one, this was Meyer's first attempt at a book and two, Tingley was not a fan of vampire books. However, while her work colleague slept on the plane, Tingley dipped into the manuscript. And to her great surprise she couldn't put it down.

She said, 'I kept thinking, "Well, she can't possibly sustain this." The whole book is going to fall apart. She's a first-time writer. I was with a colleague, and he was trying to sleep, and I kept pulling him awake and reading passages to him.

'She created this world that you want to enter right away. There is no way to predict the life of a book. You have to go with your instinct.'

Explaining the book's popularity, Meyer said, 'If you're like I was – not in the popular crowd, a little clumsy – you have Bella to identify with.'

It's hard to believe now, but *Twilight* wasn't the huge overnight success that everyone expected. 'All the signs were there,' said Tingley, 'but in the beginning they were modest. The sales kept getting a little higher each week. It wasn't a gigantic phenomenon overnight – I think people think that now, but it wasn't.'

It was only when Little, Brown released the second book, *New Moon*, that they began to think the series was becoming something of a phenomenon. Only 100,000 copies were printed (25,000 more than *Twilight*'s first print), but at that point advance copies were selling for hundreds of dollars on eBay. And, when Meyer did signing sessions, she was amazed at the numbers of people who turned up.

Tingley told *Time* magazine, 'The kids had been cutting school to get these tickets and waiting in line forever. When Stephenie came out, these girls next to me started trembling and crying and grabbing each other. It was crazy... it was like the newsreels of the Beatles or Elvis.'

And the series has become so popular that Meyer herself was the main character in a comic-book biography written about her, *Female Force: Stephenie Meyer*, published just before the release of *New Moon*.

The publishing company behind the venture, Blue Water, said, 'We get to turn the table on Meyer and she becomes the featured protagonist. And we are going to tell her story in a very fun, respectful and unique way.'

But, even before the massive success of the books, Meyer's vision was already being earmarked for a Hollywood makeover. In fact, it hadn't even been published when it fell into the hands of a very important person.

The film's producer, Greg Mooradian, said in the *Twilight* production notes, 'Part of my job as a producer is to scour the world for new material. I read a lot of manuscripts prior to their being published.

'When this one came across my desk, I just couldn't put it down. The premise of a girl falling in love with a vampire just hit me like a ton of bricks. And the book delivered on every level.'

He went on to add in another interview, 'It had universal themes, like *Romeo and Juliet*, which certainly influenced this book. It struck me this was a great movie premise – it seemed the greatest idea nobody had ever done. But, at the time, there was no way to predict it would connect with every young girl in America the way it has, that it would become an anthem for young girls as much as anything in contemporary culture.'

Unlike other writers who are tremendously precious about letting their books be adapted for the screen, Meyer displayed no such attitude. 'When I was writing the novel I saw it as a movie. It was a very visual experience, so I really wanted to see it brought to life,' she explained.

In fact, her only stipulations were that they had to keep all the Cullens in the film and they had to retain the core elements of the book series.

Delight that her book was being made into a movie turned into sorrow when, as often happens to a lot of potential movies, the film 'languished' in development hell – a term used for a film idea that has been bought by a studio but is struggling to get made.

It had all looked so promising when Paramount's then president Karen Rosenfelt agreed to make it though the company's MTV Films slate.

'Greg was so passionate, and ready to dive on his sword, knowing this would be a franchise both for publishing and for film,' she said.

However, despite the fact that a writer had been brought in to work on the screenplay, production was halted when Rosenfelt left the company. Enter fledgling film company Summit Entertainment. And it was Catherine Hardwicke who Summit turned to in order to get the book onto the big screen. Hardwicke's first job was to rework the script that had been developed with MTV in mind.

She recalled, '*Twilight* was fascinating to me, but, on the opening page [of the script], Bella is introduced as a star athlete, she's like a track star. Then there were FBI agents – the vampires would migrate south into Mexico every year, and FBI agents in Utah were tracking them. They ended up on an island chasing everyone around on jet skis.'

Not a great start. Hardwick continued, 'Bella is clumsy, she's not an athlete, she's awkward. She's like every other girl. That's why we relate to her. By the end of that script it was like *Charlie's Angels* with the FBI and jet ski. I said to Summit, "You guys have to make it like the book." So we went back to Stephenie's book.'

She had worked with screenwriter Melissa Rosenberg before, and felt her sensibilities were perfect for the series. Rosenberg, who had written the screenplay for Summit's *Step Up*, was working on the TV show *Dexter* when Eric Feig called her, asking, 'How do you feel about teenage vampires?'

After drawing up a brief outline on the movie's storyline, she was asked if she could write a script in five weeks.

She recalled, 'I said, "No, you can't write a movie in five weeks," and they said, "Well, do you want to get it made?" So, as it turns out, you can write a movie in five weeks. You do nothing else. You don't sleep, you don't pet your dog, you don't kiss your husband – you have him bring you snacks – you don't shower, and you certainly don't see friends or family.'

Talking about the appeal of the books, Rosenberg told online review website Shock Till You Drop, '[Summit] came to me, actually. I had written *Step Up* for them. They had asked me to do *Step Up 2* but I was unavailable. When I turned that down I thought I ruined my relationship with them, but eight months later they called and asked, "How do you feel about teens and vampires?" I said, "Are you kidding, I love teens and vampires." They turned me onto this book and I loved it.

'I read it over the course of eight hours – one long day – because we were moving so quickly on the film and I got caught up in it. I loved the mythology she created. Vampires are probably an overdone genre in storytelling.

'We've all seen a gazillion different vampire movies. And to bring something new to it is very difficult to do. The last person to do it well was, I think, Joss Whedon and before him Anne Rice. Now we've got Stephenie and she has reinvented the mythology while staying true enough to it that aficionados can still sink their fangs into it. I was just really impressed and delighted with her inventiveness. At the heart, the relationships and the characters she brings to it are great and that's what makes it different – who the characters are.

'I think it was MTV who was developing a script over there – I never read it, they wouldn't let me – but Stephenie said it was a good script but it didn't have anything to do with her book. I think she got very concerned about optioning it to another studio because she wanted her book to be adapted. When she went to Summit and they convinced her to let them option it she insisted on a series of things that absolutely had to be in the book. Things that could not be changed. For instance, the characters had to be the same, the vampires had to have the same skills and same limitations. We had this manifesto we started with that was a couple of pages. They sent it to me and I thought there was absolutely nothing on the manifesto that would hamper me. We've all had favourite books adapted for the screen then say, "Why did they do that?"'

'It was less trimming the fat, but condensing it.'

In a press release on 16 November 2007, Summit Entertainment announced to the world: 'We at Summit are truly excited about the franchise potential of this remarkable *Romeo and Juliet* story. Of course, you are only as good as your Juliet and Kristen Stewart has that magical combination of being a great actress, deeply appealing, and perfect for the part.'

Talking about Stewart's casting, Hardwick said, 'We spent four hours working on scenes and running after birds in the park and playing. The next day when I saw the film [*Into the Wild*, which Stewart was in], I knew, yes, it has to be. She is Bella.'

A month later they announced the casting of Edward Cullen. Erik Feig, Summit Entertainment's president of production, said, 'It's always a challenge to find the right actor for a part that has lived so vividly in the imaginations of readers but we took the responsibility seriously and are confident, with Rob

Pattinson, that we have found the perfect Edward for our Bella in *Twilight*.'

While the casting of Jacob Black wasn't heralded with the same fanfare as Edward and Bella, Lautner was delighted to get the part. In the first film, he appears in a handful of scenes, but fans of the series knew his role was only going to get bigger and bigger.

When he went to audition for the film, Taylor admitted that he had no idea what he was letting himself in for.

'When I first found out I had an audition for some *Twilight* movie, my agent told me, he's like, "Yeah, this one's kind of big." And I was, like, "I've never heard of it."

'So I go in on it, and, yeah, the director's really cool. I go back and I read with Kristen Stewart and she's really cool. Still have no idea what the project is about or how big it is. So then I get cast and I go do my research. "Oh, this is based off a book series. How big is the book series?"

'So I check it out and it's just mind-blowing. I'm just, "Oh my gosh, what am I getting myself into?" This is life-changing.'

When he bagged the part following six call-backs, the *Twilight* fans began to express concerns about his heritage and whether he was the right person to play Jacob. However, they and he learned that he had Native American blood in him.

'We learned that through [preparing for] this film. I'm

French, Dutch and German, and on my mother's side, she has some Potawatomi and Ottawa Indian in her.'

He was so desperate to do the part justice that he made sure he did his research.

'When I first went up to Portland to film, I met with some real Quileute Native Americans,' he revealed to Mediablvd.com. 'We went out to dinner with them and got a chance to talk to them. The funny thing I learned is that they're just like me. They showed up in basketball uniforms. Somehow, we got on the topic of what they like to do for fun, and they go to the beach and check out girls. It was really interesting to learn that they're just like me.'

To MTV he said, 'One thing they do that I noticed is they don't need to be told to what to do. If the trash is getting full, they empty it out. They're always helping each other. They're always there for each other. So I just want to make sure I can bring that part of Jacob alive.'

That he did, and in doing so he became incredibly close to the character: '[The werewolf side] is not like me in real life: I'm like Jacob's Native American side. I'm very friendly, outgoing, energetic and easy to talk to. But playing the werewolf side, where he's holding all this anger and stuff inside him, that'd be very different for me. I love to challenge myself as an actor.'

He said later, 'The fans would love anybody who played Jacob. I'm just lucky to be the one who got the chance.'

It was a tough shooting schedule: 'Most of our time, we wake up bright and early, go film until six o'clock at night, so all we had time for was go back, get a bite to eat together, and hit the hay for the next day. So it was quite fun, though. The cast is awesome.'

Filming in Portland – which was doubling up as the sleepy town of Forks – would largely be remembered for the weather.

Producer Wyck Godfrey remembered to *Fangoria*, 'The weather changes so quickly, it's extraordinary. Within an hour, it's hailing and you're like, "Let's run to the other set!" And then, all of a sudden, the sun comes up. And it's, "Oh, shoot! Let's run back!" It's shocking that we're on schedule. Last night, we were shooting the final scene – the prom – and they were outside dancing in this beautiful location, and there was hail falling! I was like, "I don't know that it hails in May in Forks!"

'You just find a way to fight through it. It's all you can do.'

Lautner recalled, 'We showed up for the beach scene, where Jacob is just supposed to take his wannabe girlfriend Bella for a nice walk on the beach. And it was forty-mile-per-hour winds, hail rain, the tide up to our knees.

'Wardrobe had originally picked out just jeans and a T-shirt for us, and when we show up it's pouring rain, sleet and hail the size of golf balls. So we ended up wearing three pairs of pants, raincoats, rain pants, beanies, everything possible, and I'll always remember it.

'It was my least favourite because it was kind of hard to act in. You're trying to be all serious walking her and you're almost falling over because of the wind, golf ball-size hail balls – but at the same time, it was kind of fun. It was an adventure.'

Although the part of Jacob features more in later films, in *Twilight* Lautner's main scenes are with Stewart, so it's no surprise it was she he ended up bonding the most with.

'The only people that were there when I was on set were Kristen and Rob, and he wasn't there too much. So it was basically just me and Kristen. She's very easygoing. It takes her a little bit to warm up to people. She's a little shy and reserved. Her and Rob both are. But she was very fun to be around.'

Despite her tender age (turning just 20 in April 2010), Californian native Stewart is something of a veteran when it comes to Hollywood roles. Among a number of performances, she's played the Jodie Foster character's daughter in *Panic Room*, a hippy girl in *Into the Wild*, a carnival worker in the sweet coming-of-age comedy *Adventureland* and an amateur bank robber in *Catch That Kid*.

Despite the fact that her parents are both in show business – her dad John a stage manager, her mother Jules a script supervisor – she was discovered all by herself when she was eight years old.

'I was at a Christmas performance at my school. There was an agent in the audience and I sang "The

Dreidel Song".' Suitably impressed by what he saw, he offered her some auditions.

Like Lautner, Kristen Stewart was also a minor. And Hardwicke concedes that fitting the schedule around Kristen posed a challenge.

'And this was a wild one because Kristen was a minor too, up until the last two weeks. So you start out with ten and a half hours, then you take the two hours driving one way, an hour each way to every location, then you've got the two hours in the chair – she had contacts, she had the hairpiece, the makeup. Then you have three hours of school and then you have lunch. It was five and a half hours I had her and she's in every scene. So that was its own just brutal challenge. I mean I was just kind of like, "Well how did I get into this one?"'

In fact, Kristen had to have school lessons in the very school in which they filmed *Twilight*. They had to put paper over the door glass because curious *Twilight* fans kept peeping in!

Taylor also had schoolwork to contend with, and on top of that the small matter of the wig he had to wear.

'Everyone else got the cool costumes and the makeup, the pale skin and the coloured contacts. All I got was this long black wig that reached halfway down my back. I hated it. It was the hottest, itchiest, most uncomfortable thing I've ever worn. I couldn't wait to get it off at the end of the day.'

Lautner obviously made such a big impact on set

that it wasn't long after the first cut that he was asked to come and shoot more scenes.

During reshoots, he told journalists, 'Well I am going to be in the prom scene now, at the very end of the film. At first we didn't film that, and now some people are saying they want to see a bit more of Jacob, and they want him in the prom scene at the end.'

This scene is what excited Taylor and fans of the series, because it hints at the potential love triangle of Edward, Jacob and Bella. When Jacob tries to warn Bella to be careful, Edward cuts in and leads her to the prom. He says wryly, 'I leave you alone for two minutes, they send the wolves out.'

Hardwicke explained, 'When we put the film together we realised you are missing Jacob at the end, so we put together a short scene; but it's important, because you still get a taste of that rivalry between him and Edward.'

Filming that scene was something of a vindication for Taylor, as he had pleaded with Hardwicke to put it in when he realised his favourite scene from the book never made it into the original script. He told Movies.about.com, 'When I read the script I was like, "Really, he doesn't come to the prom?"

'I think I asked Catherine about it and I forgot what she said. But I was just like, "Oh, OK…" But, sure enough, you know, they were like, "OK, we're doing it." '

There was a huge wave of interest from the film, and it was a swell that Summit began to understand fairly quickly. While they were playing down the huge media interest as the box-office opening weekend loomed, they were taking huge steps to ensure that the film wouldn't be leaked to fans.

Screenwriting magazine journalists could read the manuscript only in the office of a PR agency, and one journalist had to drive three hours to watch about 20 minutes of scene in a preview reel.

Originally meant to be released on 13 December 2008, it was moved forward to 21 November after *Harry Potter and the Half-Blood Prince* vacated that slot and was slated for release the following summer instead. The slot was a potentially highly lucrative one, as it was pre-Thanksgiving weekend – a time when audiences usually go to the cinema in droves.

It could also have been something of a poisoned chalice. Forget word of mouth, if *Twilight* hadn't found a huge audience straightaway with such a highly coveted slot, the franchise could have ended before it had properly begun.

Not that Wyck Godfrey was concerned. 'You don't go for those dates unless you know you have the goods.'

And they certainly felt they had the goods. Despite some less-than-positive reviews, it became a huge box-office hit.

Twilight fever had begun, and Taylor Lautner was very much part of it. But for how long?

chapter four

Twilight Fading for Taylor?

'Jacob is a totally different character in New Moon. *He's a foot taller and huge – and he's supposed to look 25. It's really a question of whether or not the same actor can play the role.'* – Melissa Rosenberg, *Twilight* series screenwriter

When Taylor Lautner auditioned for the role of Jacob, he had never read the books but was faintly aware of them. However, after reading them at a quick pace once he secured the part, he began to get excited about the film's potential.

He was sure the film would be a hit; he just didn't know how big a hit it would be. And he certainly didn't count on the huge fan attention that would follow.

Twilight's fanbase is a diverse one and comprises all ages and sizes. Falling under the umbrella of 'Twi-Nation', you've got 'Fan-Pires', 'Twi-Hards' and 'Twi-Moms' – and it seems they all had a soft spot for the young Taylor.

While Jacob wasn't seen much in *Twilight*, make no mistake: the character plays a huge and vital role in the series. In fact, it's Jacob, not Edward, for whom Meyer has always had a soft spot: 'Jacob is an ordinary kid who has to deal with extraordinary things that he wasn't prepared for,' she said. 'I love Jacob, because he's such a sixteen-year-old boy. I just love him as a character. He's become such a big part of the story because I had such a soft spot for him. I have been surrounded by boys, with my kids, my brothers, my father and uncles, so he was very familiar to write about.

'Originally, Jacob was just a device,' said Meyer. 'Bella needed a way to find out the truth about Edward, and the conveniently located Quileute Tribe, with all their fantastic legends, provided a cool option for that revelation. And so Jacob was born – born to tell Bella Edward's secret.

'Something happened then that I didn't expect. Jacob was my first experience with a character taking over – a minor character developing such roundness and life that I couldn't keep him locked inside a tiny role. From the very beginning, even when Jacob only appeared in Chapter Six of *Twilight*, he was so alive.

'I liked him – more than I should for such a small part. Bella liked him. Her instinctive trust and affection came without my intervention.'

Luckily for Jacob – and Lautner – Meyer's editor fell in love with the character as well, asking Meyer if they could 'get more Jacob in the story'.

Because Meyer was writing *New Moon* at the same time as she was polishing *Twilight*, she managed to go back and 'weave more Jacob through *Twilight* more centrally'. In fact, Meyer is such a fan of the werewolf that, at a push, she would probably choose Team Jacob over Team Edward. Kind of.

'I can't choose a side. I love both characters so much; it's like choosing between my children. I'll admit I have a special place in my heart for the Jacob fans, just because they're so outnumbered.'

Indeed, his *Twilight* character is so loved by the series' fans that there have been many classroom arguments as to which team they support. Of this battle between Team Edward and Team Jacob, Taylor said, 'I think that everything is kind of crazy about this franchise and that's why we love it so much and that's why the fans do as well. But, yeah, there are definitely a lot of fans who are on the two separate teams. I don't know. I mean, sometimes it gets me a little nervous because I'm trying to live up to the fans' expectations and trying to represent Team Jacob in the right way. I don't want to disappoint them, so that's why I worked so hard to not only mentally and emotionally but physically change as well for this role because this guy is some pretty good competition. So I've done a lot of hard work.'

But even Taylor wasn't to know how big the support was until cast members went to San Diego's Comic Con event to give fans a sneak preview. It's fair to say that the *Twilight* presentation was hands down the biggest hit of 2008.

Fans turned up in droves and screamed the place

down. It was only then that the cast realised what they had let themselves in for. Even when they were introduced one by one to the audience the screams were deafening. Each answer was greeted with rapturous applause, no matter how mundane the replies were to the many questions.

He recalled, 'This is a big event and there's going to be, like, six thousand fans there. We got there and it was huge. Just coming out onstage and hearing everyone scream and seeing how many people were in that auditorium was crazy.'

For Taylor, the film's premiere was one of the best nights of his life, and he's glad he shared it with a member of his family rather than just some nice-looking girl on his arm. It was the right thing to do with all the support his family had given him in chasing that dream – a dream that had become fully realised in front of the flashing bulbs and screaming.

He said before the premiere, 'I invited a lot of people but I'm having one of my grandparents come out for the movie and they're actually going to the premiere. All of my family lives in Michigan and every family member has read the books – I mean all four of my grandparents, aunts and uncles, everybody! It's just crazy cool that they love it so much.'

It's clear that Taylor has a lot of time for his fans: he and his family made a surprise appearance at a midnight book release for the final book in the series, and the kind-hearted actor ended up signing books until 2am.

For a young boy from Michigan, he can't believe the attention he receives. Every day there will be a constant visual reminder that his life has changed for ever. He always sees scores of female teenagers wearing T-shirts emblazoned with his image and the words 'TEAM JACOB'.

'It's weird to see my character's name on other people's bodies,' he recalled to Mediablvd.com. 'I guess it can get a little nerve-racking at some points, but it's just exciting for me, knowing how much the fans support this, and knowing how passionate and dedicated they are.

'I read it sometimes [what's said about him on the Web]. I'm not on the Internet 24/7 going, "Ooh, what are they saying about me? What's the latest stuff?" But sometimes I run into stuff, and I do check out some of the fan sites for the book. The fans are driving this thing.'

One fan encounter left the actor blushing, however. A middle-aged woman began to strip so he would autograph underwear she was wearing.

'I had this forty-year-old woman trying to find a way to take her panties off for me to sign them. They had my name imprinted on them. So that was kind of strange. But you can expect anything from these *Twilight* fans.

'One of the other weirdest fan things is somebody sent me a link and said, "What is this?" And it was a picture of women's underwear being sold online with "Taylor" written on it. So it was kind of weird to have women's underwear with my name imprinted on the front.

'It's funny, but about a year ago I'd talk to girls and

no one would be interested. Then when it was announced I would be in *Twilight* and everyone seemed to change their mind,' he said modestly.

Suddenly, he was hot property and he was quick to seize the opportunities given to him. He signed on to play the Christian Slater character's son Jack Spivey in the TV show *My Own Worst Enemy*. The press release for the show – in which Slater plays two aspects of his character's personality – notes the following synopsis: 'Henry Spivey is a middle-class efficiency expert living a humdrum life in the suburbs with his wife, Lily, their two kids, a dog, and a minivan. Edward Albright is an operative who speaks 13 languages, runs a four-minute mile, and is trained to kill.'

Neither of the two parts of Albright's/Spivey's mind knows of the existence of the other, thanks to a chip implant. However, when the chip malfunctions, forcing the two personae to swap with each other, things get very complicated indeed.

Because of his hectic working schedule, it was clear that Taylor couldn't juggle school life with his burgeoning film and TV career. In a 2008 interview with *Vanity Fair* he said, 'I've always been in a public [state] school until this year, actually. I am working on a TV show on NBC, and I would be missing too much school. So I tested out of high school.'

He is now taking college classes in his spare time – however little that is – in a bid to ensure he has a solid backup plan if the acting career doesn't work out.

Unfortunately for Taylor, *My Own Worst Enemy* was cancelled after only nine episodes. Taylor was disappointed but not defeated – after all he did have the *Twilight* sequel coming up, didn't he?

Well, even that wasn't a sure thing. It's hard to believe now, but there was serious thought given to replacing Taylor with another actor. The sticking point was that studio bosses feared he lacked the physical stature that comes through Jacob's transformation into a werewolf – described in detail in Meyer's books.

When he found out he that it wasn't 100 per cent confirmed, he was of course devastated. He had presumed that he would be included for all film instalments of the book – an assumption that was based on the fact that, during the audition for *Twilight*, he had made sure he did an audition with Stewart to gauge their chemistry for later films.

Taylor revealed, 'I originally met with Catherine [Hardwicke] and she wanted me to do a "chemistry test" with Kristen Stewart. We did a few scenes from the first book, like the beach scene, and then we read some lines straight out of the books *New Moon* and *Eclipse*.

'I don't remember the specific scenes, but I do know that the scenes I did showed a huge difference in Jacob's character. He goes from happy-go-lucky and friendly in *Twilight* to when he's more of a werewolf and more of an adult, all intense and grumpy. She wanted to see as much of me playing the different sides to Jacob as possible.'

The first inkling that his future in the series was in jeopardy came through the shock departure of director Hardwicke. Her exit was very much a surprise to the series' fans, as she had only recently begun disclosing her plans for *New Moon*, and the success of *Twilight* made her the most successful female director on opening weekend ever.

She said before her exit, 'I was doing a lot of research on wolves before [*Twilight*] and we had a scene with the wolves in it. So we're already thinking a little bit about [Jacob's transformation]. Then there's the stunts, and there's Italy. It's all cooking in the brain.'

Of the fears that Taylor wasn't the right physical shape for Jacob in the future instalments, she added, 'We are putting him on a medieval torture thing and stretching him. No, he's only sixteen, so he is still growing. His dad is tall, and he's working out, so you never know.'

The official reason for her departure was scheduling difficulties. Because of the huge success of *Twilight*, Summit were keen to get to work on the sequel as soon as possible. Despite Hardwicke and the studio's insistence that it was an amicable split, it was rumoured that Summit weren't impressed with her direction of the film. Certainly, it wasn't the best-received movie by critics despite its earning a huge amount at the box office.

Replacing Hardwicke was Chris Weitz – the mild-mannered director behind films such as *The Golden Compass*, *About a Boy* and *American Pie*. Unsurprisingly, diehard fans weren't happy about the changes. In fact, Hardwicke's departure caused such an angry response on the forums that Meyer issued a statement of support for Weitz. She said, 'I've had the chance to talk to Chris, and I can tell you that he is excited by the story and eager to keep the movie as close to the book as possible.'

When Summit announced the *New Moon* cast list, Lautner's name was pointedly absent. 'The casting decision in regards to the character Jacob Black has yet to be made' was what MTV News were told when they enquired about his omission from the press release.

Lautner himself spoke out about his absence from the press release: 'I think it's because, well, Rob and Kristen were the lead roles in *Twilight*, so they've got to be back. I don't know if they've officially signed – maybe they are, I don't know. They just hired Weitz, and now they're just moving down the cast. All I can say is, I'm going to be ready if my number's called.'

Talking about the situation, Rosenberg told *Teen Dream*, 'Jacob is a totally different character in *New Moon*. He's a foot taller and huge – and he's supposed to look 25. It's really a question of whether or not the same actor can play the role.'

One of those potential replacements was *Scorpion King 2* actor Michael Copon. The actor was less than subtle about his desire to win the part, posting messages on his Facebook status such as 'Michael Copon is in a *Twilight* Zone!' and 'Michael Copon is the older Jacob Black!'

Luckily for Lautner, Summit hadn't counted on the show's legion of hardcore fans who were desperate to keep him in the franchise. One post from a fan summed up the majority of the fans' opinion: 'They cannot get rid of Taylor. I don't care if he'd be a short Jacob, they just can't get rid of him.

'He played a perfect Jacob. I mean, come on! Have you seen the guy they're thinking about replacing him with! Michael Copon is such a jerk, but Taylor is a big sweetheart. If they replace Taylor I'm not gonna see anymore of the movies.'

His co-star Ashley Greene publicly fought in his corner: 'We all love Taylor. He's such a sweet guy, so sweet and I think that he gets the part. And the thing is that the girls just love him. He is the teen heartthrob... I'm hoping that they don't replace him because we love him.'

What Summit didn't count on, though, was Lautner's in-built fighting spirit. He wasn't going to give up the role of a lifetime easily. Showing the never-say-die attitude that won him the all those martial-arts championships years before, he embarked on a serious, strenuous workout regime to ensure that he matched the bulkier character described in the book.

Lautner said, 'Well, yeah, when I was filming *Twilight*, I obviously knew where Jacob's character was going and if I wanted to continue playing him correctly that I had some work to do. So, literally the day I finished filming *Twilight*, I flew back home and went to my local gym and said, "I need to pack on some pounds." '

He pledged to Weitz that he would put on the muscle before filming began and told MTV, 'I've heard a few things. I don't really know too much to comment on it. As far as I know, I haven't been told "No" yet, so it's still all up in the air.'

It was a gruelling exercise regime. 'I was in the gym five days a week, two hours a day. At one point, I was going seven days straight. I had put on a lot of weight, and then I started losing it drastically, so I was worried. It turned out I was overworking myself. My trainer told me that I couldn't break a sweat, because I was burning more calories than I was putting on. The hardest thing for me was the eating. At one point I had to shove as much food in my body as possible to pack on the calories. My trainer wanted me to do six meals a day and not go two hours without eating. If I would cheat on eating one day, I could tell – I'd drop a few pounds.

'I grew out of a lot of my clothes. I went from a men's small to a men's large.'

Lautner praised his personal trainer, saying, 'Jordan Yuam – he's really talented. He helped me a lot with this process. He's always on set, like, shoving food in my mouth. Literally, I'd be talking to somebody and he comes up with a plate. He wakes me up in the morning. He's like, "Take this protein shake." I'm like, "I'm sleeping." Yeah, I have a lot of people to thank.'

There were times when he began to have doubts

about whether all his hard work was in vain, but he kept his eye on the prize. 'I just wanted to focus on what I could control, and I worked really hard. Yeah, the gym was a major part, but I really studied the books and the character, too. And it all turned out good.'

It certainly did, with his persistence and hard work impressing the *New Moon* director. 'I'm very happy that Taylor will be playing Jacob Black in *New Moon* and that he's doing so with the enthusiastic support of Summit, the producers and Stephenie Meyer.

'The characters in Stephenie's books go through extraordinary changes of circumstance and also appearance; so it is not surprising that there has been speculation about whether the same actor would portray a character who changes in so many surprising ways throughout the series. But it was my first instinct that Taylor was, is, and should be Jacob, and that the books would be best served by the actor who is emotionally right for the part.'

Explaining their initial reluctance to recast Taylor in the role, Weitz revealed, 'The character in the second book is meant to be six foot five, let alone transform into a werewolf and all that stuff. And Taylor, having only done three days of work in the first [film], it was time to take a pause and say, "Should Taylor go ahead and do it?"

'My overwhelming feeling was, "Yes, absolutely, let's go forward with it." To me, it wasn't a very difficult decision. For Taylor, it wasn't difficult at all. He knew the character, and he embodied the character – as people are going to see in the movie.

'So it wasn't really as tense and as scary a moment as it was portrayed in the media,' he added.

Kristen Stewart added, 'The only people who were concerned and reconsidering him for the role were the suits. Chris Weitz, even Catherine Hardwicke before him, the cast – everyone on the movie was rooting for him.'

Taylor was understandably delighted with the news that he was back, telling journalists, 'My experience on *Twilight* was wonderful and I am looking forward to continuing on with the team for *New Moon*. I have been working hard preparing for the physicality that this role will require and can't wait to get started with the filming of *New Moon*.'

He added, 'I love where Jacob's character goes, and I think it would be wrong of me to say he's not my favourite character, but he honestly is my favourite character. I love him because he has so many different sides to him. You know, in *New Moon* I get to bring alive this first side that carries on from *Twilight* – his pre-transformation side where he's just this really happy, friendly kid. As soon as he transforms, he becomes this really disturbed, grumpy, fierce guy. It's disturbing.'

Not only was Taylor delighted, but so were the cast members, who had already begun rehearsals for *New Moon*.

'I'm so glad they didn't have to find somebody else – we already had him,' said Stewart. 'I didn't understand all the deliberation on whether to bring him back. But, now that's it's set, we can all rest.'

Nikki Reed, who plays Rosalie Cullen, beamed, 'I'm so proud of him. He didn't have the part. Everybody knew he was going to have to fight for this. He was at the gym twice or three times a day. He was on a nutrition and workout regime for the last year not knowing if he would be in this film.

'We were all on edge. It got closer and closer, and it was heartbreaking. Kristen and I were in Africa when we got the call saying he got the part. She's so stoked.

'I don't know if I would have had the confidence to do that, and be told no if it didn't work out. He just went in there and said, "I'm going to do the best that I can." And it paid off. I'm so happy for him.'

'He's a man now,' said Kellan Lutz, who plays Emmett Cullen.

Taylor Lautner was back for *New Moon*, but he wasn't going to be alone. *New Moon* introduces Jacob's Wolf Pack, and over the next few chapters we'll take a look at the actors who play them.

chapter five

The Wolf Pack

'I have a great compassion for young Native actors and we make it our business to find new faces for all our films. Even though a lot of actors weren't right for New Moon, I made notes – this was an amazing new talent pool.' – Rene Haynes

New Moon casting director Rene Haynes was hardly overstating the facts when she claimed just after the Wolf Pack actors were announced, 'These kids are kids whose life is going to change. They are now stars. And right now they are just getting the tip of the iceberg.

'[Rene Haynes Casting] has developed a rapport with Native peoples. Casting for *New Moon* was fantastic, because we don't get opportunities that often for young Native American actors to appear in something with the following of the *Twilight* series.'

To find Jacob's Wolf Pack, Haynes and her team searched across America. They pored over 600 video auditions and searched through their database of up-and-coming Native American actors. She also received more than 20,000 emails from wannabe actors begging for a chance to star in *New Moon*.

'I have a great compassion for young Native actors and we make it our business to find new faces for all our films. Even though a lot of actors weren't right for *New Moon*, I made notes – this was an amazing new talent pool.'

One particular open casting session in Vancouver saw hundreds of teenagers turned away because of the huge numbers hoping to get a chance to star in *New Moon*. One of the casting assistants, Bim Narine, told the *Vancouver Sun*, 'This is more than we expected. It's definitely a good turnout.'

Crucially, part of her mandate was to ensure that each actor was Native American. 'They had to have papers that proved their heritage,' said Weitz. 'And they had to be in good physical shape. It was important to the filmmakers. That is why they hired me. And that was my job.'

After an intensive and gruelling search they finally found their five actors.

'Every single aspect was successful,' Haynes told Celebuzz.com.

CHASKE SPENCER (SAM ULEY)

Although Chaske Spencer would go on to become well known for playing werewolf Sam Uley in the *Twilight* franchise, it was not the first supernatural role that he played: he had once been Count Dracula in an off-Broadway stage production.

'I like the fact that the vampire is very mysterious; they've got that skinny rock-star thing going on. I remember when I was a kid I read all the Anne Rice books and she romanticised the vampire and I thought those were really good. So when I got the Dracula role it was my first role in New York City and I thought I was really cool and I went all out with the monologue, I lost weight, I had a good time.'

A good time it may have been, but it was one that was seen by not much of an audience.

'No one came to see it! It was very humbling,' admitted Spencer. 'I was 22, and there were pin drops. But I really honed my craft and I think that is what theatre is all about. You have to show up and be present. In film you can always do another take, and you can do a scene several different ways. In theatre you can take risks and I like doing that – that's what life is about, taking risks.'

And taking risks is something that Spencer has always done.

Born on 9 March 1975, in Tahlequah, Oklahoma, Chaske Spencer grew up in a number of places, including Montana, Maine and Idaho. After graduating at Clearwater Valley High School, he went to Lewis-Clark State College in Idaho, only to leave after a year in a bid to pursue his acting dream. He had been bitten by the acting bug after performing at

Lewiston Civic Theatre. Having originally dreamed of being a photographer, he was now seeking a career in front of the camera rather than behind it.

With $100 in his pocket, he booked a one-way ticket to New York in a bid to make a name for himself. He worked a number of odd jobs, including bartending and waiting tables to pay the bills. This working environment would prove useful for Spencer, as he would spend his time observing his customers – watching their mannerisms and their dialect.

He finally got his break after a year in New York, when he landed the part of the Count in *Dracula*. 'I was really desperate. I didn't want to be a teacher, even though I had considered it because both my parents were. I'd thought about being a photographer; really, I just didn't know what I wanted. Luckily, I was young and dumb. Why else would I have come to New York like that with a hundred bucks to my name?'

He thrived working on stage, but he had always dreamed of being seen on screen after going to the cinema as a five-year-old and watching *The Empire Strikes Back*. As well as being shocked at finding out that Darth Vader was Luke Skywalker's father, he was struck by how cool Han Solo was and was desperate to emulate his idol.

The play wasn't a hit, and Spencer was particularly distressed with a review in the *Village Voice* that described him as 'the self-doubting Chaske Spencer'. 'I was crushed,' he remembered.

However, one person who was impressed with what she saw was casting director Haynes, and she remembered him when she cast the 2002 Native American drama *Skins*.

Between the play and the role in *Skins*, he received acting lessons from one of the top teachers in the business, David Gideon, a former director of the esteemed Lee Strasberg Theatre and Film Institute.

Skins was a great experience for him. His may have been a small part but one of the scenes saw him act alongside a veteran talent and future *New Moon* co-star, Gil Birmingham. However, he realised that he still had a lot to learn.

'There was one scene, which ended up being cut out, where Nathaniel [Arcand], me and Gil are at the dinner table. I had a few lines. I was being way overdramatic; I was giving way too much, like I was on stage. I really had to tone it down.'

However, Arcand joked, 'What impressed me working with Chaske was that he didn't screw up his lines and he didn't step on my lines… kudos, my friend, kudos.'

He next starred in the 2003 TV movie *Dreamkeeper*, and provided voice duties on the game *Red Dead Revolver* a year later, before starring in the Steven Spielberg-produced miniseries *Into the West*.

Away from starring in films and TV, he is a spokesperson for the charity organisation United Global Shift, which 'aims to reduce poverty and create sustainable communities', according to his website.

Charity is something close to his heart: 'I'm originally from Montana and Idaho and a lot of people there live on Native American reservations, so there is a lot of poverty. I understand the importance of when someone can't afford something. I remember my dad, who also coached football, would buy some of his players football shoes when they couldn't afford it.

'He wouldn't say anything, he wouldn't make it known, but he would buy them football shoes and they would have them in their locker. So I learned that from my father.'

He also set up his own production company, Urban Dream, with his manager Josselyne Herman and film producer Ted Kurdyla.

He is also hugely into making music, with his acting résumé listing many of his musical talents, including singing and playing bass, piano and drums. He has played drums since he was 15, and would often head to the band room at his school and play along to Metallica songs to relieve any tension.

He also lives in a house in New York with the bass player of the cool New York band the 5 O'Clock Heroes, Adam Morse.

Just as he was beginning to become frustrated with his career so far, *Twilight* came calling. Chaske was desperate to land the role, not only because it was a perfect career break, but he felt this was a different portrayal of Native Americans from those usually seen on screen.

'It's written for First Nation people or Native Americans or American Indians, whatever the new PC word is,' he said. 'It helped out a lot. But, then again, the way the book is written isn't a stereotypical Native role. That's what I found really interesting about the *Twilight* series, is that it could have been anybody. It just happened to be Natives and I like that. I really like that, how she took a contemporary outlook on these characters. It was really a breath of fresh air for all of us, the Native actors. We've been trudging away in films, TV and theatre and we can do other roles. We have done other roles that weren't designed for Native people but no one has ever seen them.

'When we got to this it was so nice to not put on the feather and the leather and the buckskin. There's nothing wrong with that – I take pride in the roles I've played – but it was just a breath of fresh air to say that, yes, we could play these contemporary roles. It was so nice to cut the hair, too. Yes, we can do other things. Look at us. And we're a pretty good, talented group.'

Spencer actually read for the character of Jared first, before landing the role of Sam. He told *Vanity Fair*, 'It was one of the weirdest auditions I've done. We put it on tape, and usually the process is: you meet the casting director, get a callback, then you meet the producer and director. This just went straight from tape. I auditioned for all of the parts of the Wolf Pack; they called me back and told me what part I had. Also,

I didn't really know who [the character] was because I didn't know much about *Twilight*.

'Then I figured it out and said, "Wow, that's a really good part." It's amazing. I've never gotten a part like that before.'

Casting director Rene Haynes remembered, 'It was a very long process. It was up and down, up and down. But he floated to the top. He's an emerging young actor who has paid his dues. This isn't just someone we picked off the street. He's studied and is ready for this.'

She added, 'He's someone I feel is going to be a star. I have cast him before. He's always done lovely work. It's awesome to know that it's time for this young actor to have a great breakout role like this.'

When he landed the role he sank to his knees and thanked God. He had to ensure that he kept the fact that he was playing the character under wraps from the media for nearly a month and a half. To ensure there was no leak, he never even told his family and friends.

He told *Radar Online*, 'It was hard. It was really hard because I told my friends I got booked on a pilot so I would have an excuse to go to Vancouver. I told them yeah, I booked a pilot and I'll be up there for a little while. I told my parents the same thing.

'I kept it pretty close. It was really cool. I guess that's how the guys in the Wolf Pack really bonded, because we couldn't tell anyone so we just talked about it amongst ourselves. All the excitement and what we're going through, the workout. I guess that's how we bonded, the workouts and, plus, it's like a brotherhood of secrecy, so we had to keep this big secret and we just talked. It was good to vent to one another and bounce ideas off each other. It was really hard.

'The paparazzi got us in a restaurant, they took our picture with Chris Weitz and Taylor. Then about a few days later it came out and I got to tell all of my friends. They were like whoa, man, what's up, Spence, why didn't you say anything? My mom and dad, they were just excited.'

While Spencer was bemused by the media attention already, he was also to experience the negative side of so much focus on him. When someone gets thrust into the spotlight, it leaves them open to nasty allegations, and private moments in their life are scrutinised, twisted and turned.

The US gossip mag the *National Enquirer* claimed that Spencer checked into rehab in a bid to get clean of drink and drug troubles. Spencer was quick to clear up the story, admitting that he did go to rehab, but it was long before *New Moon*. In a statement, he said, 'For those of you that read that I was in rehab, I wanted to make sure you heard the truth from me directly. Yes it is true, that I was in rehab; however, it was over 19 months ago, long before *New Moon* was even on my radar. It was a pivotal time in my life where I was lucky enough to have supportive friends and family to help me get healthy.

'I am grateful that I have been clean and sober now

for 19 months and cannot imagine my life if I had continued using drugs and alcohol. Almost everything else that was written about this is blatantly false and we are exploring our legal options. That was my past, and I am thankful that I had the opportunity to create a new future for myself. I encourage anyone who is in a similar place to seek support from their friends and family and know that without them, I would not have had the chance to be where I am now.

'I want to thank all of you for the support you have shown, and continue to show. I appreciate each and every one of you.'

Spencer would generally find the fan attention a positive thing, revealing, 'It started for me March 5 when I got cast in *New Moon*, and I don't know when it's going to be done. It's been like a wild ride. We got cast and there was already sort of a buzz about us. As it got closer, you kept feeling the build-up and the build-up, and all of a sudden at the premiere, it just exploded. It was like a rock-star moment. This is what we've been waiting for. People are telling us our lives are going to change. And they have.'

To get into character he read *New Moon* as well as *Eclipse*, because there's 'a lot of backstory to my character'. Like Lautner, Spencer had to hit the gym to make sure he was the right shape to play the leader of the Wolf Pack convincingly. Unfortunately, he had only three weeks in which to do it.

'They got us a trainer and really started throwing us

into the work, into working out, which was with a gentleman who helped out on *300*. I was pretty psyched about that; it was really tough. I was [already] in shape, but, when he got his hands on me, it was a whole different beast altogether. I put on 25 pounds in those two months. It just happened – one day, I stepped out of the shower, took a look at myself, and I didn't recognise my own body.'

He may not have recognised himself, but he would be one of the few who didn't. *New Moon* would launch him into the big time.

ALEX MERAZ (PAUL)

Alex Meraz was born on 10 January 1985. He was a creative child desperately seeking an outlet for his talents. And he would find several things that would interest him, including martial arts, dancing, drama and art school.

He said, 'I went to an art school in Arizona called New School for the Arts, and I was basically drawing nude models at the age of thirteen. Initially, I wanted to be a professional painter, and eventually I got a scholarship to the San Francisco Art Institute. However, I ended up not taking that route because I realised that art was something I could always do. There were other things I wanted to do with my body that I could only do for a certain amount of time – like dancing.'

When he was five, one of his older brothers would take him to hip-hop clubs in Arizona where he DJ'ed, and he just stared in amazement at the wildly creative dancing on display. 'I'd watch all these kids dance and I was hooked,' he said. 'My first discipline, as far as dance goes, was breakdancing. I hung out with a lot of street kids in Arizona and got into the whole hip-hop scene. One of my brothers was a DJ, so he would take me out to clubs. At that point I was five or six and a lot of those places were twenty-one or older, but I'd watch all these kids dance and I was hooked.'

However, it would be drama that he would feel the most natural doing. It wouldn't be until he moved to San Francisco, though, that he would be bitten by the acting bug.

At his high school, his drama teacher saw potential in Meraz, but at the time he felt acting was just performing in 'crappy musicals'.

Meraz added, 'I didn't want to do that. It wasn't until I moved to San Francisco that I met my mentor, [the actor] Raoul Trujillo, who saw me dance, thought I'd do so well in film and got me my first acting gig.'

He made his debut in 2005's *The New World*, followed by an appearance in a short film called *Two Spirits, One Journey*.

In *The New World*, he was one of the Powhatan core warriors. 'That's kind of where he got the bug,' said Trujillo. 'It was an incredible experience.'

Trujillo remembered that, at the wrap party for *The*

New World, Meraz's dancing caused a stir – with the film's leading man, Colin Farrell, particularly impressed. 'Colin was just sitting and watching cross-legged all gaga going, "Oh my God."'

Trujillo added, 'The camera loves him. Everywhere we go people are always saying, "Good God, who is your friend?" This is only going to be scarier now.'

Following *The New World*, he then appeared in *We Shall Remain* and *The American Experience*. He nearly landed a part in Mel Gibson's grizzly blockbuster *Apocalypto*, but ultimately just missed out. Trujillo explained, 'Mel felt he didn't look Mayan enough, which was silly. I don't look Mayan either, but they put a prosthetic nose on me and I looked plenty Mayan.

'If there's anyone I have known in my life that deserves this, it's Alex,' added Trujillo. 'He's worked his ass off in the time I have known him. He never lets up.'

After discovering that he was up for an audition, he embarked on an eight-hour drive to his mentor's New Mexico ranch on his birthday weekend in a bid to work on what he would do for it. Talking about the experience, Meraz told *Vanity Fair*, 'I got a breakdown for an open casting call – they were looking for Native actors – and I submitted my stuff and luckily I got a role. One of the casting directors was kind of the Native American liaison. I had been cast in another one of her films. I sent her my original casting tape. She liked it, but she thought we could do better. So she brought me into LA, I gave it a whirl, and I eventually got the role.

'First I went out for Sam Uley, the Wolf Pack leader. We did this whole scene from the book that they took out because they weren't releasing anything from the script. So it was a scene where we're at [the character] Emily's house and we discover Victoria – who's a vampire – had been killing on the reservation. So we figure out who's been killing all these people and hikers and bikers on the reservation, and we figure out it's a vampire. So it was that scene, and I had to kind of like play a quarterback and tell people what they needed to do. The hard thing about that, in the book, Sam is described as six foot four and with a deep voice. You know, like a leader. And I'm five eleven. I don't have a deep voice. So I was trying to act like something bigger.

'Then luckily enough, Joseph [Middleton, casting director] said, "Let's try this." And he gave me one single line. He gave me a [lead-in], "Come in Bella, we won't bite." And I had to look at the camera and say, "Speak for yourself." But the way I did it, it was so naughty. I blew a kiss, gave a little wink. Like, really naughty. And it was based off of that one line that I got the role of Paul.'

He learned he had got the role when he was in the kitchen, 'about to make some food. Then I got the call and was really surprised. I initially went out for another role, so I was heartbroken at first because I didn't get that role. But then they told me I got the role of Paul, which I hadn't even auditioned for. At that point, I was relieved I got something.'

Meraz explained about the character, 'Paul is the "bad boy" of the Wolf Pack. He comes across as volatile, but I think he's misunderstood. He is just very proud of being Quileute and is unapologetic about being a protector for his people.

'I looked at books on wolf-pack mentalities and how the chain of command is governed by looks and postures, so I wanted to use some of those attributes in playing my role.'

Rene Haynes explained why he was cast: 'Alex is a professional dancer. He is definitely a rising star in the Native American experience.'

Like the other actors who make up the Wolf Pack, the appeal of seeing 'Natives portrayed in a contemporary setting' appealed to him. He added, 'It's not a period piece. I had been doing other independent films and things like that where I'm in a breechcloth running around on horseback hooting and hollering. There was something just really cool to know that it's a global sensation, and now Natives are going to have the spotlight.'

And he was quick to address concerns that the film was being disrespectful of the Quileute tribe, saying, 'It serves them in that it takes things from the mythology and their creation story and combines it with fantasy.

'But it's not completely accurate. Part of their creation story is that they came from wolves, but they can't change back. That's one of the things that the Quileute are protesting. But I think it serves them because it's giving them the spotlight. It informs people of the tribe. Now tons of people are coming to La Push [the reservation] to see people from the Quileute tribe. I think that's great. I've talked to the other Wolf Pack members and we've discussed that we'd like to go to the actual reservation and speak with some of the council members and pay homage. That's kind of the Native way, anyways. You can't just take something: you have to give back as well. So that's something we plan on doing at some point.

'I personally was shocked when I heard that the books had a huge Native component in them. It was the whole part of the Wolf Pack, and I didn't know how big the Wolf Pack was until I read about it. I was just shocked that people were interested, you know what I mean? So I thought, "Wow, that's amazing. I totally want to be part of something like that."'

It was his Vietnamese–American wife Kim who introduced him to the books as soon as she found out that he was up for a part. Raoul Trujillo said, 'His wife is the one who has read all of those books. And she's the one who said, "Look, you have got to get into this. This is perfect for you. You're the one." '

Meraz fell for his wife, Kim, when he saw her showcasing her salsa moves. 'Hips don't lie,' he said. Instead of rings for the wedding day, they got lines inked on their fingers, the reason being, 'Tattoos are extremely sexy on women,' he said. They also have a young son called Somak.

With a devoted wife and a loving family, Meraz wasn't going to be to swayed by the fan attention that was sure to come his way. However, he recalled that he was very curious to see what the series' fans thought about his casting.

He said, 'I read a couple of things. The first month, you obsessively go online and Google yourself. And [director] Chris Weitz, he gave us a bit of advice. He said, "Alright, I've got to say this. I know you're going to do it: just go online for the first month and get it out of your system. Google yourself, but then stop. Because then, what's going to happen is you're going to be getting really mad about something that a twelve-year-old is writing online."

'And it's true. The first month, I did it, and I got a lot of good response. Then I started getting other ones that were just wild. Like, "He totally shouldn't be Paul. He doesn't look like Paul. He looks like too much of a nice guy."

'Well, I just thought, "It's called acting, sweetie." That's when you start talking back to your computer, and you're like, "Wait a minute. This is wrong."'

He added, 'I knew it was a huge phenomenon. And then you worry: "I hope they embrace me." Because the other downside to that is, the fans, they've been reading these books, and they fantasise what the characters look like already.

'So if you don't match up to their ideas of who the characters are, they'll derail you. They'll badmouth you online. It was like that with Rob [Pattinson], too. They didn't like the way that Rob looked. But I had an understanding, which was once they see it in context, once the movie comes out, they'll get it. They won't be imagining anything else. They're going to see what is there. Because that's what happened with *Twilight*. They hated Rob; then they saw the movie, and now Rob's the biggest heartthrob ever.'

KIOWA GORDON (EMBRY CALL)

Embry Call is described as one of Jacob's 'wingmen'. They started as best friends, but Embry grew distant after his transformation, because he couldn't share his secret with best pal. However, when Jacob himself is transformed, their relationship goes back to being the way it used to be.

Call was originally played by Kris Hyatt in an uncredited appearance in *Twilight*. But, for *New Moon*, the role went to Kiowa Gordon.

He was born on 25 March 1990. Growing up in Arizona, he is the second youngest of eight children. His mother Camille, an actress, certainly had her hands full with a household that big.

Gordon said, 'Our tribe is called the Hualapai, and we are in Northern Arizona. We sit on top of the Grand Canyon and used to live there [on the reservation] about ten years ago. We take frequent trips back.

'When I was growing up, my mom tried teaching us [the language], all my seven siblings and I. But we just laughed at her, because it sounded funny to us. Now, I'm kind of sad that I couldn't learn it, because it's a dying language. So, hopefully, I'll get to learn it sometime soon.'

Gordon was unsure whether he wanted to follow his mother into acting. Indeed, his efforts in drama class at Cactus Shadows High School resulted in only a C grade. He managed to land a small role in *Black Cloud*, which his mother starred in, and one in *Skinwalker*.

Coincidentally, he is part of the same church as Meyer – the church of Jesus Christ of Latter Day Saints, or the Mormons. And it was Meyer who played a big part in getting Gordon a role in the film.

He said, 'They had an open casting call here in Phoenix, and I auditioned. I was going to church with my mom out in Cave Creek, and Stephenie Meyer goes to church with her. She kind of helped me out on that one. She told production, I think, and got me some sides to do the audition. She took a look at me and thought I could play one of her wolves.'

He had read the first book as a school assignment, and knew just how big the series was. To make sure he had a chance of securing the role he spent an hour with an acting coach going over the basics.

He had seen Alex Meraz at the audition, but there

was very little small talk from the young and shy actor. He was just desperate, if nervous, to land the part.

However, two weeks later his mother would get an email that would change her son's life. It said what Gordon's large household had been longing to hear: he had secured the part. Gordon was particularly delighted with the character, because, 'It's not just leather and feather, it's roles meant for Caucasian actors.'

Once he spoke to director Chris Weitz, Gordon was on his way to LA to get a cyber scan in a bid to perfect his body movements needed for computer-generated imagery, or CGI. His Wolf Pack co-star, Bronson Pelletier (Jared), explained, 'We get cyber-scanned, which is basically a huge Xerox of every angle and inch of us, so when we change into the wolves it has that full effect. Each wolf has [the actor's] own individual eyes on them, and that is pretty cool.'

He also got a shock when he was asked to cut his hair. 'I've had long hair since the seventh grade, to my shoulders. Our hair has to be short when we become werewolves. I had no idea they were going to cut it. Oh, man!'

He bonded with his wolf co-stars when he went to Vancouver to rehearse and get in shape. 'During the first three weeks I hung out with the Wolf Pack. We worked with a personal trainer. I gained five pounds. We all bonded and became like brothers.

'They got us a personal trainer, and we just went to the workouts and got to know each other. We saw each other's strengths and pushed each other's buttons; we really bonded during that time.'

But he would also bond with the rest of the cast: 'We had a big dinner together, the whole cast and the director and the producers. And we all got to know each other and just become friends, basically. Now I have some friends for life. It's really awesome.'

And it wasn't long before Gordon found out just what being in a *Twilight* movie meant to the fans. 'I guess I've been welcomed with open arms. A couple weeks after getting announced out there to the public that I got the role, a girl actually tattooed my name on her back with a paw print!'

And, if that's what was happening *before* the cameras even started rolling, he could only imagine what it would be like when the film came out.

TYSON HOUSEMAN (QUIL ATEARA)

Tyson Connor Houseman was born on 9 February 1990, and is a Native American descendant of the Cree nation.

He grew up in Edmonton, Alberta, where he would spend a lot of his childhood usually fending off his three younger brothers, who would 'team up against me when we play fight and stuff like that'.

He was an avid skateboarder after being taught by his uncle, and later tried his hand at learning snowboarding, long boarding and surfing. Houseman attended high school at the Victoria School of the Visual and Performing Arts.

Like Chaske Spencer and his Cullen family co-stars, Houseman is a talented musician. 'I've been playing for five or six years, but I'm self-taught and I've never performed in front of anyone, so I don't really see myself as a musician. Maybe if I ever get the guts to play in front of people, then I might consider following that path. But my heart really does lie in every aspect of art. In high school I had a huge passion for photography. When I was a little kid I loved to draw…

'Art is an extremely important part of my life. I see art everywhere and in everything. I think that's why I also enjoy photography so much, because I can find a certain type of beauty in everything that I see, and I need to capture that beauty. Acting is an art and it is also something I really enjoy. As long as I am pursuing an art and growing as an artist, then I'm happy.'

He added to Examiner.com, 'All throughout grade school, my notebooks had more doodles in them than actual notes. Art is an extremely important part of my life. I see art everywhere and in everything. I think that's why I also enjoy photography so much, because I can find a certain type of beauty in everything that I see, and I need to capture that beauty. But, as an artist, I try to be as ranged as possible. Acting is an art and it is also something I really enjoy. After I went to the open casting call for *New Moon* and got the part, I felt that an amazing opportunity was given to me, and how could I turn that down? This has opened up so many doors for me, and I plan on following through with it.'

Not that acting was something completely new to Houseman: he performed a number of stage productions in high school.

'I was in a production called *The Laramie Project* in which I played various characters. It was an ensemble piece, so there were around 22 actors playing roughly 200 parts in total. But not 200 each – that would be terrifying. I have also played Romeo in *Romeo and Juliet*. Actually, I have played Romeo twice already in two different productions.'

While he wouldn't do any stage work outside of his school, he admitted, 'I think they ended up on my acting résumé because there was nothing else I could put on there and I wanted to fill it up a bit.'

It's only after *New Moon* that he is now taking acting classes – and in fact the *Twilight* sequel was his first ever audition. 'It was actually an open casting call, and I found out about it from a friend. I thought that it would be a good experience to have, and I never once expected that I would get it. But I did the open casting call, and I got a callback the next week.

'When they sent me the lines I had to learn for the callback, the casting director told me that there were two different scenes, one really long one and another really short one. He told me I only had to do the short one and they wouldn't have time to do the long one, and it wouldn't even be in the film. But I learned the long scene anyways and when I did the callback I did the short scene and afterwards I asked if I could do the long one too, and they said yes. A week later I got a call saying I had gotten the part.'

While he never actually knew what he was auditioning for – the open casting call just said it was a major motion picture – Houseman quickly realised that it was for *New Moon*. 'When I got to the casting call it was filled with hundreds of *Twilight* fans carrying books and T-shirts and everything *Twilight* related. So when I saw the crowd I knew it was for *Twilight*.'

Like the rest of the actors who make up Jacob's Wolf Pack in *New Moon*, he had to prove he was of Native descent. 'At the open casting call they had to come down the line-up and make sure everyone was of Native descent, or they wouldn't let them audition. I think it's great that they cast Native people for the parts, because it allows us to fall into the character much easier. There is a deeper level that we can relate to the character on.

'When I first got the role I didn't think about the fanbase. Then somebody told me, "Do you realise there are thousands of teenage girls that are gonna be freaking out about this?" I was like, "This is gonna be a little weird."'

Houseman would play one of Jacob's best friends and his second cousin. Initially, he can't understand why his best friend is acting strangely. However, when he finds out that he's turned into a werewolf along with

werewolves

v

vampires

THE WEREWOLVES

For *Twilight* fans around the world, Robert Pattinson is the vampire of their dreams.

Above: Rob meets and greets his fans at the première of his film *Remember Me*.

Below left: With his *Remember Me* co-star, Emilie de Ravin.

Below right: Looking very dapper in his costume, Rob is pictured on the set of *Bel Ami*.

Kellan Lutz (who plays Emmett Cullen) and Nikki Reed (Rosalie Hale) get playful at a *The Twilight Saga: New Moon* fan Q & A session in Los Angeles.

Above: Jackson Rathbone (Jasper Hale), Ashley Greene (Alice Cullen) and Kellan Lutz pose together at *The Twilight Saga: New Moon* film première in Los Angeles, 16 November 2009.

Below left: Peter Facinelli (Carlisle Cullen) and Elizabeth Reaser (Esme Cullen) together at the MTV Movie Awards 2009.

Below right: Ashley and Kellan sign autographs for fans.

Peter Facinelli is always grateful for the support of his wife, Jennie Garth, and three daughters, Luca Bella, Lola Ray and Fiona Eve.

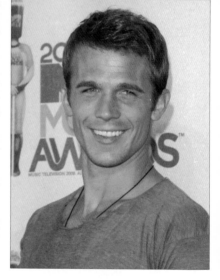

Above: Rachelle Lefevre (who plays Victoria), Robert Pattinson, Nikki Reed and Kristen Stewart make an appearance in Toronto.

Below left: Edi Gathegi (who plays Laurent) poses with Chris Weitz, the director of *The Twilight Saga: New Moon*.

Below right: The villain of *Twilight* is James, played with gusto by Cam Gigandet.

The Volturi are a powerful vampire coven who live in Italy and are regarded as royalty by other vampires.

Clockwise from above left: Michael Sheen plays Aro, Christopher Heyerdahl plays Marcus, Dakota Fanning is the delicious evil Jane and Jamie Campbell-Bower is Caius.

Robert Pattinson is Edward Cullen, the best representative of the Vampires.

Taylor Lautner is Jacob Black, the best representative of the Werewolves.

Above left: Taylor and Bryce Dallas Howard, who replaces Rachelle Lefevre as Victoria in *The Twilight Saga: Eclipse*.

Above right: Taylor attends the Nickelodeon Kids Choice Awards in March 2010.

Below: Signing autographs for fans at the *New Moon* première.

Above: Taylor gets to mingle with all the big name stars now, including Academy Award winner Hilary Swank.

Below left: To keep in shape, he continues to be very active and into playing sports.

Below right: Taylor has perfected the brooding look.

Above: Bronson Pelletier (Jared) and Chaske Spencer (Sam Uley) goof around at the Berlin photocall for *The Twilight Saga: New Moon*.

Below left: Alex Meraz (Paul) can't escape the paparazzi even when out shopping.

Below right: Chaske Spencer cleans up nicely for the première of *The Twilight Saga: New Moon*.

Chaske Spencer (Sam Uley), Tinsel Korey (who plays Emily Young, Sam Uley's imprinted fiancée) and Gil Birmingham (Billy Black, Jacob Black's father) together at the Red National Film Festival.

Above left: Alex Meraz with his wife, Kim.

Above right: Kiowa Gordon, who plays Quileute wolf pack member Embry Call.

Below left: The only female shape-shifter is Leah Clearwater, who will be played by Julia Jones in *The Twilight Saga: Eclipse*.

Below right: Boo Boo Stewart will play Seth Clearwater, who has an instrumental role in *Eclipse*.

Human, Vampire or Werewolf – it doesn't matter when the cast are all good friends! Taylor came out to support Kristen and Dakota for their new film *The Runaways*.

The two main men who epitomise the debate: Edward V Jacob, Robert V Taylor, Vampire V Werewolf – which side do you choose?

the rest of his friends he is happy to become one of them so he can be with his pals again.

While his character, Quil, doesn't change into a werewolf until *Eclipse*, he made sure he attended the workout sessions with the rest of the pack to bond with his new friends.

Acting may not have been Houseman's true love, but he was beginning to be smitten with it.

BRONSON PELLETIER (JARED)

While Chaske Spencer is the leader, Alex Meraz the hunky one, Kiowa Gordon the shy one and Tyson Houseman the quirky one, Bronson Pelletier is the cheeky one.

He said, 'The vampires are very serious, but when we got on set that's when the party started. The Wolf Pack were the wild ones. They called us the crazy monkeys. On set it was like, "Oh, the werewolves are here!" There goes the neighbourhood!

'Each character I portray I like to bring a little of myself to. I brought my jokester side to Jared, so he's a little bit of a jokester but a little more mature than the other wolves.'

Born on 31 December 1986, the Canadian youngster was a hyperactive child, so it made perfect sense for him to channel that energy into performance, and he would go on to cause a stir on two Canadian TV shows. The first was the action drama *Dinosapien* in

2007, and he played a lead character in *Renegadepress.com*, which follows a group of youngsters running an e-zine. That show deals with a series of risqué topics, including drug use and sex.

Its co-creator, Robert de Lint, said, 'Everyone is forced to deal with the legacy of their family dynamic – parental abuse, blended families, illness and loss, childhood memories that haunt adult parents. These are the issues that all Canadian teens face in their transition from childhood to adulthood. It is important to acknowledge and address these stories.'

While Pelletier enjoyed working on the show, he was desperate to star in a movie. 'With film it's hurry up and wait and with television it's hurry up, hurry up, hurry up,' he explained. 'You have to do ten scenes a day and bang them off… time is money. Film is so chill and slack and you get to put more of your creativity into it.'

And he was to get his wish, because not only was he to star in a movie, but it just happened to be one of the most eagerly awaited sequels in years.

When he found out that his audition had been successful, he was so delighted that he ended up nearly ruining it before he began. 'I was so psyched, I was so pumped. I ran into this random gas station. I had to tell someone else, "Yeah! I just got a part in a movie!" I was so happy!'

The only problem was, though, that, when the female petrol attendant asked him what the film was, he couldn't tell her, because he had signed confidentially agreements. So he had to rush out without answering. In fact, he had no real idea what the series was about, anyway. 'I watched the movie [*Twilight*] and read the books after I got the role. I'm kind of glad it happened that way because I probably would have been more nervous in the audition.'

But when he did finally get acquainted with the source material, he was delighted with both the books and the first movie. 'It's really opened a lot of doors for aboriginal actors. Before this, every role I've ever gotten was for an aboriginal character. I'd go for roles that would say "for all ethnicities", but what they're pretty much saying is, "We want a Caucasian guy or a black guy." One or the other. Now that we've actually finished this movie, it's opened up a lot of doors for aboriginal actors. There aren't a lot of us out there, let's be honest.'

And he was determined to make sure that he did the part justice: 'You definitely gotta be a good role model, no matter if you're aboriginal or not. I gotta be careful with what I say and what I do, because I know a lot of younger aboriginal youth are looking up to me, and I didn't really expect this to happen, but it kinda comes with the job.'

His management company, Carrier Talent Management, announced to the world on its website that Pelletier was joining the cast of *New Moon*: 'Congratulations to Bronson who scores a lead role in the highly anticipated *Twilight* feature film sequel *New Moon*.'

Talking about rehearsing before the cameras rolled, he said, 'Pretty much what we do is work out. We work out, we work out and we work out. We work out together; that's what strengthened our camaraderie and turned us into the pack. It only took an hour or an hour and a half for one of us to break the ice – it was probably me. We'd just rag on each other. I tend to be the guy who likes to goof around and make fun and joke, so it didn't take long for that to happen.

'I'd worked on other stuff before, so you know you have to have chemistry with somebody or it seems forced. But, with these guys, it's organic and natural; it's real. We're not putting on a charade. I plan on knowing these guys for the rest of my life. They're great guys and real people. I call them up every now and then when we're not working, just to see how they're doing or if we have problems. If I have a problem, I'll call these guys up and they'll help me out.'

chapter six
New Moon Rising

'You turn the corner and there would be one, two, three, four hundred teenagers standing there. It got to the point where the stand-ins were signing autographs!' – Chris Weitz

There is another member of the werewolf family that we can't forget, and it is Billy Black, who is played by Gil Birmingham.

Talking about his character, the veteran actor said, 'We're both down with the kids. We both have genuine compassion for the human condition. We both recharge our souls with Mother Nature, and we both keep it real.

'Billy simply loves his son and his family [tribe]. Billy is the wise tribal leader, who, because he isn't a werewolf, understands the dangers and complexities of the "tentative" peace between the Cullens and the Quileute tribe. He knows the dangers that the Cullens present to Bella and the others. Billy is the glue that holds the tribe and its traditions together.'

New Moon presented a welcome reunion for Birmingham and Chaske Spencer (Sam Uley).

Spencer said, 'I was very happy to be working with him again. Out of the whole cast I'm pretty close to Gil. We worked several projects together; actually, all of the projects I've done have been with him. It was very top-secret when I was getting this role. He didn't know when I was cast but he was very happy. We go out to dinner; we can talk about what's going on. He gives me advice. I love the guy; he's like my older brother. One of the nicest men you'll ever meet. I like working with him. He'll be there for me. In *New Moon* we just bounce stuff off each other and I'm very excited to work with him again'

Filming on *New Moon* was something of a huge shock not only to the new cast members, but to the *Twilight* ones as well. During filming of the first movie, the stars were startled when they saw fans peering through the trees or lining up in numbers behind closed-off sets eager to sneak a peek at the screen version of their favourite book.

The shoot in Montepulciano, Italy, was something different, however. 'Every teenager who could get there from any part of Europe was there, and it was like *The Birds*,' director Chris Weitz recalled, referencing the famous scene in the Alfred Hitchcock movie when the heroine finds herself surrounded by a mass of birds just waiting and watching.

'You turn the corner and there would be one, two,

three, four hundred teenagers standing there. It got to the point where the stand-ins were signing autographs!'

He added to *Time* magazine, 'The streets were filled with fans. The nice thing was that they weren't interested in hampering the filming at all. When you asked the crowd of 1,000 people to be quiet, they were absolutely silent. But then when you finished a take, there would be a round of applause, which doesn't happen on a film set.'

New Moon is the story where the love triangle that is Bella, Jacob and Edward heats up. And Taylor Lautner was determined to ensure that the chemistry between him and Kristen Stewart was just as believable as that between her and Pattinson. They would spend lots of time together at each of their LA homes and bond over dinners and watching DVDs.

'It was very important for me and Kristen to grow very close,' said Taylor.

Talking about their relationship, Kristen added, 'It's lamely cute. I love that kid. I would do anything for him.'

Spencer raved about Kristen's and Taylor's work ethic: 'It was really good. Everyone has a different way of working; I learned that a long time ago. Kristen is an old pro – she's been working since she was a child. She comes ready to go. She's got her character down; she knows what she wants to do. She's very open to ideas as well. She's ready to play. Taylor is the same way. He's been working since he was a kid as well. I have a hard time thinking of him as a kid, because he's got that man body, but he still has that baby face. The thing is, they're both good people, that's what I love about them.

'They're both egoless. We did a scene in Emily's home and Kristen got all her scenes done and she stayed. She stayed for us to do all our close-ups. You don't *have* to stay: you can get a stand-in to come in and say all your lines. But she stayed the whole time. And it was a long day. So that shows what kind of integrity and what a trooper she is. I really tip my hat to her on that. Taylor is working. When he's not doing his scene he's getting his muscles pumped, with all of us; we're all doing push-ups between scenes. Those two, I like working with them. They come in, they're ready to go, but they also know when to have a good time. They keep it light on the set as well, which is really good for an actor. You have to stay relaxed on set.'

However, getting the love triangle right proved tricky for the film's screenwriter, Melissa Rosenberg. 'I think we've found the balance, because the other thing you're doing is setting up another relationship, which will lead you into Book Three, which is a triangle and introduces the new addition. But I will say it's a challenge because you want Edward in there as much as you can. And what's true is that [Bella's] entire storyline throughout the movie is really about him – there are other elements, but they're all motivated by having lost him or feeling the pain of having lost him. You have to keep that alive, which actually ended up being not as difficult or as big a reach as I initially feared.'

Talking about the love triangle, Taylor said, '*Twilight* develops the relationship between Edward and Bella. In *New Moon*, Edward leaves, and Bella needs someone to bring her out of this depression she's in, so she turns to her best friend, Jacob. It looks like it could go past friends. Bella's very confused. Jacob wants nothing more than to be more than friends. He wants Edward to get out of there so he can move in for the kill.

'Bella's torn. She's still in love with Edward, but she's kind of fallen for Jacob, too. When I read the books, I feel bad for Jacob, because he can't have what he wants. I understand Jacob's pain but also Bella's pain – how she's confused and torn between the two.'

Stewart added, 'She loses what basically gives her the drive to do anything in her whole life. She loses the man she's in love with, but she also loses her entire life plan, and she's so young to have to be forced into a decision like that. It's just a glorified, elaborate version of the worst breakup you've ever been through. All of a sudden you question everything. All of a sudden you know nothing and you're dropped in the middle of a frozen ocean.

'This is a severely emotional movie. That's the one big difference. This movie is not about discovery or falling in love, which is sort of just an intense emotion, but this is like low and there are high points for her, too. She's a manic-depressive basically. To have a character be able to pull her out of that, it's a hefty feat, which I think we pulled off. But for me, like, I don't know. There was no difference. It was just sort of heavier and it was more to think about. It's a more mature part strictly because she's older and she has more to deal with. A lot more is introduced. The whole world of the werewolves [is] coming alive.'

Taylor loved playing Jacob in this movie, but he found the emotional moments to be intense. 'When I was reading the books, I felt so bad for Jacob's character,' he explained. 'But now that I'm actually living him, I feel way worse. Bella's toying with Jacob! I don't care if she's ripped between the two guys – I feel so bad for Jacob because she confused him. One moment she'll want to kiss him, and the next moment she's ditching him for Edward. I mean, yeah, I understand where Bella's coming from, and it's a crappy situation for all of them. But I feel really bad for Jacob.'

Taylor and Kristen had to flex their muscles to ensure that one of the book's more comical moments was included in the film.

Mike Welch, who plays Mike Newton in the film, revealed to MTV, 'Kristen and Taylor had to lobby to get this one scene in the film that wasn't originally in – and I am for ever indebted to them for that. There's a scene that's in the book, the three-way date between Jacob and Bella and Mike, where Mike ends up getting sick, and it's just very awkward.' The scene did end up making it into the movie and helped to turn up the heat on Bella and Jacob's relationship while being sweetly funny at the same time.

Straightaway, Taylor found that working on *New Moon* was going to be far different from his work on *Twilight*. Not only is he in it more, but he also realised just how demanding and tough it can be playing a character who goes through different changes, while having to shoot the movie out of sequence.

Taylor explains, 'He's a lot different than he was before. He transforms mid-story – in the first half, he's *Twilight* Jacob. I'm wearing a wig. My character's very clumsy, outgoing and friendly. When he transforms into a werewolf, he becomes something very different. It's like I'm playing a split personality. Which is tricky, because sometimes I've had to play pre- and post-transformation Jacob on the same day of filming.'

Of course, the main talking point was Taylor's physical transformation – and not only among the media and *Twilight* fans. His new physique shocked even his cast mates.

Ashley Green, who plays Alice Cullen, gushed, 'It's insane! I was going through my phone and looking at all the pictures, and there's one from the wrap party that we did here after the first one and it's incredible. I was like, "Taylor, did you see this?" He was like, "Oh my gosh." He gained thirty pounds. He's not a little kid any more.'

'He's really buff,' beamed Kristen. 'He definitely is. It took him a lot of time. If I had seen the Taylor who did

Twilight and compared him right now with the one doing *New Moon*, he's an entirely different person physically. I mean, it took him so much time. He's so devoted.'

Birmingham, a former bodybuilder, said of Taylor's physical transformation, 'He worked tremendously hard between *Twilight* and *New Moon* to bulk up, and it paid off. I'm impressed by the discipline and commitment that Taylor has to acting and to his work at such a young age. He will have a long and successful career.

'When it comes to Taylor, you have to like him. He is so young, yet he is such a talented and well-grounded young man. I hope we can work together in movies outside of the *Twilight* films.'

Talking about Wolf Camp – which was essentially a workout regime for the actors playing the wolves, Taylor said, 'It was like a basic training. I had been going to the gym before I went up to Vancouver, and just to keep in shape I go to the gym regularly; but when we got there it was a whole different beast altogether. They got us a trainer, and he had helped out the actors in *300* get in shape.

'It was really cool, me and the other guys, the wolf guys, we were pretty jacked that we were working out with the guy who was affiliated with *300*. I think we were more excited about that than anything else. So what they did is he threw us into circuit training and muscle-confusion workouts and we hit it pretty hard for about an hour and a half. First thing in the morning that's what we'd do. And then we just eat all day. It's pretty much four to six meals a day plus three to four protein shakes a day as well.'

The Wolf Pack's involvement in the film, as well as the introduction of Jacob's newly acquired physique, meant there were many male topless scenes.

'I wonder if I might have gone one shirtless scene too many,' said Weitz. 'Of course, once they turn to wolves, any clothes they're wearing split apart. It's an economic incentive for the disadvantaged Quileutes that they do not have to keep going to Target to buy new T-shirts.

'It's not pleasant for the actor, but they have all been good-natured,' added Weitz. 'They show up on location in drenching, cold rain and I say, "OK, off with the robes."'

Of the weather, Meraz complained, 'It's really cold in Vancouver and, you know, I have no shirt on. And sometimes not even shoes. I think the real acting is coming in and trying to act like I'm warm!'

Taylor recalled, 'I won't lie, it's a little uncomfortable because we're in the Pacific Northwest, and it's like 35 degrees [Fahrenheit] and you're wearing cut-off shorts and that's it. Everybody else is bundled up in several layers of clothing, shivering, and I'm just wearing nothing.'

The Wolf Pack worked out constantly on set between shots, and there were plenty of one-upmanship battles.

Meraz said, 'We are pretty much half-naked the whole

time, running around and lurking. We had to watch what we ate all the time, and before we started filming a scene we could all be on the side of the set with the dumbbells, lifting and curling and doing pull-ups.'

Talking of himself and Taylor, he revealed, 'We have to play such active roles in this movie, so we had warm-up. He did a flip, I did a flip. We were going back and forth, and he was giving me a run for my money. Finally, I gave up because my legs started hurting. I'm not seventeen like he is!'

Chaske Spencer said, 'You should see us on set! It's so bad! We're shirtless throughout most of the movie and we're constantly doing the push-ups and the sit-ups between takes. We look in the mirror and say, "OK, I can probably work this a little bit more, maybe fifty more crunches. I can lose that. I look at my biceps and check out Taylor's." It's funny, it's really funny. The other cast members laugh at us. It's pretty hilarious. I've never been so body-conscious until I landed this role.

'Between takes we'll do push-ups and they keep dumbbells on set. We're constantly working out. [The key] is muscle confusion – using the same muscles but with different routines. I've been eating six meals a day: fish, chicken, vegetables and protein shakes. It'll be nice to be a couch potato again.'

And it wasn't just the Wolf Pack actors who were competing with each other. Spencer revealed to *Radar Online* that one of his main rivals is Robert Pattinson.

'He did Vampire Camp! I don't know what his workout regime was but he would show up before or after us because we were on two different shooting schedules during *New Moon*, and most of the vampires, I met them for dinner once but then boom, we all went our separate ways to work. I would hear the trainer say, "Oh, Rob lifted this much weight", and I'd say, "Really?"

'There was this competition one day we went into the gym[.] [W]e have this rowing machine and I really busted my ass and I got a high record on it and I was like, yeah, beat that! Because the wolves are really competitive with each other in the gym. Then the next day I came in and Rob beat me by four seconds! Then filming was done and I never got to go back and try to up that.'

And, in fact, Spencer couldn't wait to begin work on *Eclipse* so he could break Pattinson's record!

He added, 'Rob would come in either before or after us. I like that, I like that we're separated from them: it builds the tension. You'll see the chemistry on screen. I think that's why they kept us wolves together, because the chemistry will come out on screen; you can't fake that. Same with the vampires: when we're on screen with them you'll see the chemistry – we're supposed to be competitive against them, resent them for who they are as vampires.

'I think that will come across. But we don't resent them in real life. They're really nice. That's what I love about the cast, they're really nice, everyone comes to play They're ready to work, they're good people. It's one of the cool things about this production, I don't think anyone really expected it to be this big of a hit, so we're all just wide-eyed and wow.'

Kristen Stewart believes that the introduction of the Wolf Pack gave the film a huge burst of energy. 'The way you see the Cullens walking around in their wardrobe, and the way their scenes are all set up, it's all very reserved. But there's something about the wolves, even when they're in a short scene, that makes it such a different movie. The Wolf Pack guys were like a lot of energy, they were always doing dance-off matches and wolf cries. It's a completely new world that has been introduced, and it's warm and fun and a little more frisky.'

Talking about his chemistry with Tinsel Korey, who plays his screen love interest, Emily, Spencer added, 'She's a sweetheart, I love that girl. What we did was we went out for coffee and we talked to build some chemistry to sit and get to know one another. When we got to filming it went really well, it went really easy. Of course, you meet someone and the next day you're kissing them. It's a weird profession. You can't fake it.

'She's one of my really good friends. I call her up. I can put her on my top five, actually. I text Alex and Kiowa. We talk to each other because we're all going through this together. Tinsel, I like her because I can talk to her in ways that I can't talk to the other guys.

It's almost like we are becoming that family in the book. Tinsel is a good actress and a talented, talented woman. I like her music. We would just hang out and talk, go to dinner, shoot the breeze.'

Meraz also has a scene where his character Paul gets slapped in the face by Bella, prompting him to change into a huge wolf. Meraz explained the angry side of his character: 'He's compulsive, you know. He kind of goes with the flow, but he's volatile, but not in a "I like to hurt people" way. He's very proud. He has a thick sense of pride, and he really wants to protect the reservation, and she's bringing nothing but trouble. So, in that scene, I'm thinking in my head, "Do something to make me change, so I can kill you." Just do something, because I'm itching to kill her. She's a nuisance, a problem. That was the way I did it in the scene, and of course she hits me, and that's enough to change me.

'We did one rehearsal, said our lines, and we were good! The next day, we shot it and experimented – one time I tried grabbing her throat, which she was not fond of – and we played around with it. The director gave us good stuff to do, and it was what it was.'

Meraz was glad that the scene finally ended, as 'she started finding a home for that fist on my face. It was getting really close!'

While Jacob's Wolf Pack were new to the franchise, they weren't the only ones. There was another vampire family introduced. The Volturi are a powerful vampire clan, with Aro the leader.

The critically lauded British actor Michael Sheen plays Aro, and won high praise for his performance. 'I think he's quite brilliant and conveys an extraordinary intelligence. Aro is, on the surface, a very gracious and friendly vampire, but beneath that he is a tremendous threat, which I think Michael Sheen can absolutely convey,' said Weitz.

Sheen said, 'The first day of filming, we did the 18th-century stuff and then one of the modern scenes. It was a lot to deal with the wig, and contact lenses all day and the makeup, but it was fantastic. These sets are amazing. And the look of everyone is so strong, so it was great to just kind of get right into it straightaway.'

The chameleon-like Sheen – who has twice portrayed former Prime Minister Tony Blair – will be remembered also for his role as a werewolf called Lucian in 2003's *Underworld*, which starred Kate Beckinsale.

'It's nice – now I can, you know, bring out the other side of me. The vampire side, rather than a werewolf side. I feel a bit like a traitor, that I've swapped sides. No, it's nice. I'm glad. The vampires get to wear much cooler clothes, in *Underworld* and in this, so now I get to have a nice bit of tailoring instead of, you know, raggedy leathers. The best thing about playing a werewolf is, you don't have to worry about getting dirty. If it's a lunchtime, I can have a lie-down and it doesn't matter, because, you know, I'm supposed to look rough. But, as for this, I'm supposed to look perfectly tailored and groomed and clean all the time, so I can't sit down or anything, because I've got all this white makeup on. I'm wearing black clothes. So, I've got to be really careful that I don't get covered in stuff.'

Dakota Fanning plays Jane, a member of the Volturi clan who has the ability to torture people with the illusion of pain. She said of her character, 'It's definitely different from anything I've ever played, to get to play someone who's a little evil for once.'

The talented young actress spoke publicly about her hopes of getting the part before she officially signed on – a sign that she was very much a fan of the franchise.

'I haven't read all the books, but I've seen *Twilight* and I'm a very big fan of the cast. Pretty much all my friends are big fans, so it's been great.'

Talking about Fanning, Sheen said, 'I think Dakota may look the most unsettling. So angelic yet so weird. Like an evil Red Riding Hood.'

Fanning's next project saw her star with her *New Moon* co-star Kristen Stewart in the rock-star biopic of Joan Jett, *The Runaways* (2010). And one scene sees her sharing a kiss with the actress. 'I really enjoyed doing that subject matter for the first time in a biopic, because it really happened – it's not just a made-up story about a fifteen-year-old kid running wild. It's a true story of her evolution from good Valley Girl to bad rock'n'roll princess.'

Another member of the Volturi was British actor Jamie Campbell Bower, who played Caius. He was forced to apologise to the film's bosses for 'misleading people' following a joke to a reporter that he is 'completely naked' in the film. He had said to MTV, 'We all just sit there completely naked for one scene. It's me, Michael and Christopher [Heyerdahl] – we just sit there, naked.'

Weitz was quick to placate shocked fans, however, saying, 'I would like to put everyone's mind at rest and let them know that the Volturi are not naked. Jamie has what you might call a dry sense of humour and almost managed to convince me – which is why he is such a good actor. Anyway, be assured that, even though we do want the look of Volturi to be a bit of a surprise, they are always – as in the book – fully clothed.'

After *New Moon*, Weitz became the second director to leave the franchise, with horror director David Slade taking control of *Eclipse*. When asked if Weitz would return for *Breaking Dawn*, as was mooted in the media after the release of *New Moon*, producer Wyck Godfrey said, 'I think everyone would be happy and excited if he came back, but I don't think it's going to happen.

'We're just focused on the treatment and getting that right. At that point, we're going to see who's available and who's appropriate. It's such a complicated book because you have the emotions and the intensity of the love story – so you need somebody who's just a wonderful director of actors – and yet it's really complicated from an action and visual-effects standpoint. They've got to have both tools in their kit.'

chapter seven

A Howling Success

'They all started screaming as soon as we walked off the bus; the whole time we were answering questions they just kept screaming and screaming. It was so surreal for me.' – Kiowa Gordon

For director Chris Weitz, *New Moon* was a triumphant success and a fitting reminder of his talents after the lukewarm reaction to 2007's *The Golden Compass* – an adaptation of the first instalment of Philip Pullman's award-winning *His Dark Materials* trilogy of novels.

Despite its literary credentials, estimated $180 million budget and a cast comprising Nicole Kidman, Daniel Craig and Eva Green, the film failed to charm critics or cinemagoers. 'It's one of the great sadnesses of my life that it didn't turn out the way I intended it,' he remembered.

New Moon's success must have turned out exactly how he wanted, however. He noted, 'To me, it has a lot less to do with vampires and werewolves than with really identifiable emotional situations. Bella has a choice between the loving friend who's nearby and the distant unattainable object of her affections.

'That's a pretty common scenario, and, unfortunately, so is being dumped. I know: I've experienced it – pretty much anybody except the incredibly lucky has experienced it – and the supernatural element of things just allows for a degree of wish fulfilment. We can play out these scenarios on a grand scale.'

While Pattinson and Stewart have struggled somewhat with the huge fan attention, Lautner seemed born to be famous. For her part, Stewart has moaned about the paparazzi attention, telling *Dazed and Confused*, 'They just wait for you. It's insane. I went to the wrong place this morning and this person's like, "Hey Kristen, I think you're in the wrong place!"

'Normal nineteen-year-old people in this world f**k up and make mistakes – they're late and almost get in car accidents all the time. It just happens and it's normal and it happens they pull over into a parking lot and I can't back out of it, because it's crowded with people shouting things like, "Hey Kristen, you lost? Are you smoking pot? Are you f**king Robert Pattinson? You know, we have a call sheet, and you're supposed to be at the production office now."

'And that's when I'm like, "Oh, my god! How in the hell do you have a call sheet?"'

Pattinson added, 'I was getting really paranoid. But then I realised that if tomorrow I say, "OK, I've had enough we're stopping everything," it won't change anything. Might as well try to accept it and stay zen, as I have no control over it. It's not always easy. But whining won't change anything.'

Taylor, however, has a different attitude to fame. His family has made sure he was aware of his burgeoning media attention. 'My friends and family send me links to fan websites. It's pretty cool.'

And, when Pattinson and Stewart experienced the huge crowds at 2008's Comic-Con (a big conference celebrating all things popular culture) in San Diego, it was young Taylor they turned to. 'Actually,' he said, 'both he and Kristen have come up to me and asked, "How do you not freak out? What do you do?" And they're all sweating. I tell them, "I don't know. I mean, this is fun!" But they're all disappointed, like "Oh, OK." They're funny.'

And 2009's Comic-Con event saw Taylor become one of the main acts and he handled the big stage brilliantly, telling fans, 'I worked really hard to transform Jacob's body so I could portray him correctly for you guys. I hope you guys are pleased when you see the results.'

But, with the focus more and more on Taylor, he's starting to see the other effects of fame. While it's great to experience the occasional rush of attention, at a premiere, say, or other big event such as Comic-Con, it's a different thing entirely when it becomes a daily occurrence.

While promoting *New Moon*, Lautner said of his fans, 'They're very intense, but it's cool that they're so dedicated and so passionate. They're the reason we're here doing this sequel. So I'm thankful for the fans. I like meeting them. But, yeah, they're pretty intense. Sometimes it becomes a little overwhelming.

'We've met many different fans: the criers, who come around quite often; the hyperventilaters, who stop breathing and have to have a medic come. We've definitely seen some passion.'

However, there is a negative side to fame, as Taylor would discover. A cruel hoax on the social networking site Twitter claimed that he had died from a cocaine overdose at a Hollywood party.

Talking to MTV in 2009 about the paparazzi attention, he said, 'There are twelve cars that camp outside my house. You can't ever really get used to it, because it's not normal to have people snapping pictures of everything you do. You just have to try not to let it affect you.'

Luckily, his feet are very much on the ground; he still hangs out with his friends from school, his parents drive him to the set and until not long ago he still relied on a weekly allowance. Lautner said, 'Kids still looked at me as Taylor because they knew me from before. You gotta remember who your friends were before you got famous.

'My parents wouldn't allow it,' he said, talking about how he would never get too full of himself. 'That's not the way they brought me up.'

His dad, Dan, added, 'We had no idea what was gonna happen. We tell him, "You have no idea what's gonna happen tomorrow, so enjoy today. Have fun." '

And he's certainly having fun, often linked romantically to a series of female celebs. One constantly mentioned is guitarist–singer Taylor Swift. Another he has been linked to is *Zoey 101* actress Victoria Justice. They were snapped in Vancouver while he was filming *New Moon*. However, Justice insisted, 'I'm not dating Taylor. We became good friends while auditioning for *Sharkboy and Lavagirl*,' she explained.

Teen actress Selena Gomez was another one he was linked to. Gomez, who has dated Nick Jonas in the past, has had tongues wagging after she and Taylor were spotted constantly together. Even more tellingly, she has been seen with Taylor's parents and his sister.

Ashley Greene spoke of their friendship: 'I think she's so cute and I think he's so cute. They should date.'

However, Gomez said, 'He's one of my good friends. [But] I'm single, definitely single. He is so sweet. Taylor has made me so happy. I didn't know I could be that happy... He's a great guy but I'm 100 per cent single and I'm going to keep it that way for a while.

'Kristen was staying in my hotel. He would visit her, so we were constantly running into each other in the lobby – and we ended up meeting. We would go out to lunch and dinner, but I knew he had paparazzi following him and I had paparazzi following me,' she explained.

'So we literally just wanted to hang out, go bowling and stuff, and it went a little too far, I think. People were getting a little crazy about us... but it was fun – I went to Vancouver thinking I was going to focus on my work, but instead I got to meet him, and it ended up being the best thing ever.'

In fact, Gomez is very much in the Team Edward camp after watching *Twilight*. 'I can totally see the Robert Pattinson thing now, that's for sure!'

In one of the more bizarre rumours involving the *Twilight* cast, it was claimed that Pattinson was becoming envious of Stewart and Lautner's budding relationship! Lautner was quick to brand the love-triangle rumours 'crazy'.

However, the rumours about him and Taylor Swift never seem to end. They met while working on the romantic comedy *Valentine's Day*. But they're not the only high-profile actors involved in the film. The staggering cast list reads like a who's who of Hollywood stars including, Julia Roberts, Emma Roberts, Anne Hathaway, Jessica Alba, Jessica Biel, Jennifer Garner, Shirley MacLaine, Bradley Cooper, Ashton Kutcher, Topher Grace, Hector Elizondo, Patrick Dempsey, Eric Dane, Carter Jenkins, Jamie Foxx and Queen Latifah.

Emma Roberts was such a big fan of the *Twilight* films that she hung around on the *Valentine's Day* set to see Taylor Lautner at work, and she also revealed what the two Taylors get up to in the film. 'They just had to make out. That's all I saw. Then I left. They were both really cool. I hung out with them a little bit.'

While Lautner refused to talk about his relationship with Swift, his *Twilight* co-stars were more than happy to talk about her. Chaske Spencer said, 'She really has gotten everyone's attention lately but it's for a good reason – she is as talented as she is pretty.' Christian Serratos said, 'She's a really, really fun girl who becomes like your instant BFF [best friend forever].'

Meraz nearly put his foot in it, however, when he slammed Lautner's new film on his Twitter page. 'Sorry Taylor but the movie *Valentine's Day* looks lame and desperate. It cries out, "Look we have all the biggest starz in 1 movie pleez watch!"

'P.S. it has nothing to do with the talented actors in the movie. I just don't like the producer and director's "get rich quick skeem" nuff said.'

However, he was quick to apologise on his Twitter page, when he realised his comments had caused a bit of fuss in the media.

The film's director, Garry Marshall, confirmed that the pair dated. And it was filming the kissing scene that sealed their romance. 'I always start with the kissing scene. The first thing they did was kiss. The first three [kisses] were nice. By the fourth I think they started going together. I don't know what the hell happened, but somewhere in the fifth or sixth take they were dating.'

Away from his celeb female encounters, Lautner's two-year relationship with his former classmate Sarah is his longest love affair. And he hasn't ruled out dating a fan in the future.

'I think one of the most asked questions is, "Would

I ever date a fan?" Well, this is an easy one. I don't look at people as fan, star or celebrity. When I look at a girl, they have to have the things that are important to me and it doesn't matter what they do or how well known they are. Actually, how well known they are doesn't matter to me at all.

'I look for someone honest, loyal and someone who can be a dork. I don't want anybody too uptight and trying to impress me. If they're just a dork and really outgoing and fun, then that works for me.'

During the break between *New Moon* and *Eclipse*, he had to maintain the weight he had put on, so it meant, yet again, endless trips to the gym. But, because Lautner was reaping the rewards of *New Moon*'s success, it meant lots of meetings and very little time to stick to his rigid eating schedule. 'If I have meetings all day, I'm running around downtown and I don't have time to [eat].'

The solution was to have bags of beef patties and mushy sweet potatoes packed in bags for him to eat in between meetings – which is of course a pretty surreal visual for any *Twilight* fans who happened to see their idol outside of a building eating from a little plastic bag!

The constant physical training seems to have taken its toll on Lautner, who moaned, 'My motivation was the movie and the fans. But I don't want to become known as just a body. If I had to choose, I would never take my shirt off again in a movie, but I guess that's not very realistic. I certainly won't be *asking* to do it, though.'

While Taylor was firmly in the spotlight, the other Wolf Pack actors could be excused for feeling a little envy. Not so, according to Chaske Spencer, who insists they have all bonded after 'Wolf Camp training' and the subsequent *New Moon* shoot. 'We are just really good friends now. It was a really good learning experience. Taylor had his own trainer and was hitting it pretty hard at his gym. Training was an hour and fifteen minutes a day of pure pain! The wolves would hang pretty tight and often go out to lunch together after working out. We'll all call each other from time to time and text each other and see each other at TwiCons [fan conventions]. So it's like we never left [each other].'

After shooting on *New Moon* had finished, Spencer took some road trips to clear his head.

'When I came back from shooting *New Moon* my friends said, "My God, you've just gone gigantaur!" I like that. It's good to look at your arm and say, "Wow, that's mine!" Sometimes I don't even know what to do with my own body. I'm like a thirteen-year-old kid who just went through a growth spurt.'

But he is grateful to his trainer for getting him into shape for his character Sam, and it has shown him how to treat his body better. 'I know this sounds so bad and so vain, but the trainer actually has changed my life. I go to the gym a lot more, I watch what I eat, it's changed my whole lifestyle. After we wrapped I shook the hand of the trainer and I thanked him so much because it actually changed my life. I'm more active now. I want to go do things. I want to do some mountain climbing, I want to run a marathon, and it's just opened up a whole new door in my life. I'm really thankful for that.'

Taylor Lautner and Tinsel Korey would donate time to man the donation lines for the Hope for Haiti telethon, which was held to raise money for victims of the huge earthquake that stuck Haiti in January 2010.

Korey was asked to write a piece about the experience for MTV. Here's what she wrote:

Like a lot of you I sat watching, wishing I could pack a bag and go there and help. I found myself wishing there was more that I could do.

Some people on Twitter were apologizing for how they only gave a little, to which I want to say: It's not how much you donate – it's that you did. Every dollar counts, every e-mail counts, every phone call counts. It all helps.

What was beautiful about the evening was not any specific individual performance. To me, everyone put their heart on the stage and sent a vibration of love to the cause.

What was amazing is that the telethon even happened; everyone put aside their personal agendas and joined together to make this event a successful one. George Clooney said at the end that the thank-you shouldn't be sent to him, but to everyone who contributed. So thank you to everyone who contributed in whatever capacity they could.

So, what now? Time for bed, Haiti will be good now, right? Nope. This is just the beginning. Please keep spreading the word. Organize events in your school, work or community centers; raise money and create awareness. Anyone has the ability to make a difference if they'll just try.

While Lautner was becoming an old hand with the attention fans were heaping on him, the rest of the Wolf Pack were new to this level of adulation. Said Meraz, 'It's so surreal, I mean, I'm feeling it right now! On the film sets of *New Moon* and *Eclipse*, I feel safe. It's like you're in the centre of the hurricane, but outside is where it starts to get chaotic. I would say that, in the last few days, I started noticing that I'm in this huge franchise. I'm going to be in one of the biggest movies of the year, and it's a little surreal, frightening and exciting all together. It's like one big roller-coaster ride.'

Kiowa Gordon recalled the crazy fan hysteria when the cast attended Comic-Con in 2009: 'It was crazy. They all started screaming as soon as we walked off the bus; the whole time we were answering questions they just kept screaming and screaming. It was so surreal for me. I've also gone to my own things – like I've gone to this unity conference out in New Mexico where Native American youths gather and share their tribal affiliations and all that awesome stuff. And [Twilighters were there and] they went crazy.'

Alex Meraz added, 'I've been doing a lot more interviews. I was a little more intimidated by it all about four months ago when I finished wrapping *New Moon*, but I've been doing smaller interviews and going to red-carpet premieres and things like that. I've gotten used to it; I call it my new "norm". But a few months ago I was pretty terrified. It was shocking to me. Now it's part of what I have to do. This franchise demands it. I had to do classes – PR classes – just recently. That kind of strengthened all that! I just try to have fun and be myself.'

The boys were certainly having fun, with Spencer remembering, 'I had a girl faint on me. And then the criers. And then the cougars – the Twi-Moms – always come after us. That's been very surreal, because we've had phone numbers slipped in our back pockets. It's like we're the Beatles.'

If proof was needed that the Wolf Pack were a close-knit group, it came with the short gap between the end of *New Moon* and the start of *Eclipse*. After they had been thrown together and thrust into this wild and crazy journey, Spencer missed them when they were gone. He would walk down the streets and find himself longing for the day when he could once again work out in the gym with Tyson Houseman.

When they finally did meet up again, there were, he recalls, 'lots of high fives, going out for lunch and dinner'.

chapter eight
Eclipse

'It's got action. The action keeps building, so I enjoy that.' – Taylor Lautner

As with *New Moon*, there would be plenty of drama *before* the cameras on *Eclipse* would roll. First, the fuss was over who would direct this third movie in the series. And there were some unusual names being mentioned – including former child star Drew Barrymore.

'I'm one of the directors being talked about, which is great because I'm a director now,' confirmed Barrymore.

Barrymore's directorial debut was the high school comedy *Whip It!*, which stars *Juno*'s Ellen Page. Another mooted was Spanish director Juan Antonio Bayona, who earned rave reviews for the 2008 horror tale *The Orphanage*.

Talking about the directorial choices, Kristen Stewart urged, 'As long as they get someone who's invested, as long as they get someone who cares. It's so above me, but I think that both are good choices in their own way. I'm sure that they'd be great. Drew's been doing this her whole life, and she's pretty cool.'

It ended up not going to either of those two, and David Slade was hired to direct *Eclipse*. Slade is no stranger to vampires after his impressive directing turn on the truly scary *30 Days of Night*. In that film, though, there were no 'vegetarian' vampires in sight! It was a very full-on action film.

Meyer said, 'I am thrilled that David Slade will be directing *Eclipse*. He's a visionary filmmaker who has so much to offer this franchise. From the beginning, we've been blessed with wonderful directorial talent for the *Twilight* saga, and I'm so happy that *Eclipse* will be carrying on with that tradition.'

Summit Entertainment's Eric Feig beamed, 'Stephenie Meyer's *Eclipse* is a muscular, rich, vivid book, and we at Summit looked long and hard for a director who could do it justice.

'We believe we have found that talent in David Slade, a director who has been able to create complex, visually arresting worlds. We cannot wait to see the *Eclipse* he brings to life and brings to the fans eagerly awaiting its arrival.'

Slade didn't get off to the best start when *Twilight* fans learnt that he once Twittered that he would prefer to be shot than to watch *Twilight*. He was left red-faced when he was offered a chance to direct the third film shortly after those comments.

To rectify the matter, he said, 'When I made these comments, I had neither seen the film nor read the books. I was promoting a comedy short film that I had made for Xbox and every pop culture subject matter was seen as a possible comedy target. I was being silly and none of the statements were from the heart.

'Of course, I have seen the movie and read the books and was quickly consumed with the rich storytelling and the beautifully honest characters that Stephenie Meyer created.

'I would like to reassure everyone involved that I am invested in making the best film that I am humanely capable of, and that I am acutely aware of the power of the original books we serve.'

Slade also responded to concerns that his two films – the brutal revenge paedophile thriller *Hard Candy* and the aforementioned *30 Days of Night* – didn't showcase a director who can handle the more romantic elements of the franchise.

'Even though people think I'm a really violent and unpleasant person, I actually do have this romantic side to me.'

Producer Wyck Godfrey maintained that they had made the right choice. 'Ever since I saw *Hard Candy*, I was obsessed with him as a filmmaker,' he said. 'That's a female-point-of-view movie, and it's very different than the *average* female-point-of-view movie. He's also done tons of videos that are female-friendly, and he has some teeth to him too, which I think is good.'

This time, for Taylor Lautner there would be no worries over whether he was to stay in the series, which is great news for him, since *Eclipse* is his favourite book: 'I like that. It's got action. The action keeps building so I enjoy that.

'So I think I enjoy that but also the fact that *Twilight* sets up the romance between Bella and Edward, and then Bella and Jacob's friendship grows in *New Moon*. But in *Eclipse* it's actually the three of them physically together and we have to team up and make this decision to try to be friends to protect her. I think that is like the ultimate high point of the series where it's the love triangle in *Eclipse*. So I'm excited to get going.'

Talking about the hot love triangle in the third film, screenwriter Melissa Rosenberg noted, 'The third book is about the triangle, and this is the episode where Bella chooses between Edward and Jacob. She's chosen when we start the movie, but then she has to go through a process of elimination. She starts by choosing from a teenage, immature place – "That's what I want" – but then she really has to look at that choice, because everything and everyone is forcing her to look at that choice, and she has to make that choice from a very mature place and really looking at the consequence of this choice.

'The whole movie is really about choice and consequences, and I think that requires some very delicate handling. You're talking about some very subtle emotions and you really have to track that, and it comes to looking at both these guys as a viable option.

'And in looking at both lifestyles and what they offer as options, it's really about "Who am I and who am I going to be? What do I want for my life?" It's a very mature question to ask, so finding that answer will require some exploration.'

While Lautner was spared the axe from the second film, Rachelle Lefevre was not so lucky. The actress, who played Victoria in the two films, was dropped because of scheduling conflicts – that was the official reason, anyway. Lefevre, however, hit back at the suggestion that her involvement on the low-budget film *Barney's Version* alongside Paul Giamatti was the reason for her exit.

Furious, she released a statement saying:

I was stunned by Summit's decision to recast the role of Victoria for *Eclipse*. I was fully committed to the *Twilight* saga, and to the portrayal of Victoria. I turned down several other film opportunities and, in accordance with my contractual rights, accepted only roles that would involve very short shooting schedules.

My commitment to *Barney's Version* is only 10 days. Summit picked up my option for *Eclipse*. Although the production schedule for *Eclipse* is over three months long, Summit said they had a conflict during those 10 days and would not accommodate me. Given the length of filming for *Eclipse*, never did

I fathom I would lose the role over a 10-day overlap. I was happy with my contract with Summit and was fully prepared to continue to honour it. Summit chose simply to recast the part. I am greatly saddened that I will not get to complete my portrayal of Victoria for the *Twilight* audience. This is a story, a theatrical journey and a character that I truly love and about which I am very passionate. I will be forever grateful to the fan support and loyalty I've received since being cast for this role, and I am hurt deeply by Summit's surprising decision to move on without me. I wish the cast and crew of *Eclipse* only the very best.

Out went Lefevre, in came Bryce Dallas Howard, who was actually the first choice to play Victoria, revealed Hardwicke. 'I cast [Rachelle], so I wish they could have worked out something. I wasn't involved in the negotiations so I don't really know the inside story... Either of them would have been good.'

Howard admits that she has a hard job ahead pleasing die-hard *Twilight* fans, saying, 'We'll see. The jury is still out, because Rachelle really created an incredible character and is exquisite. I feel like the uproar that occurred was really appropriate, because part of the joy of seeing a franchise, it's almost like a television series. You've seen the actors grow with the franchise. And [her] unavailability was really, really, really unfortunate. She won that role for a reason. I hope to honour everything that she created.'

And, talking more about joining the cast of *Twilight*, she added to Examiner.com, 'I was really struck by what an incredible group of young people are in that franchise. Their friendships are so genuine, and they really ground each other. And there is a lot going on around them. There's a lot of attention and scrutiny, but I'm truly moved by how solid they've remained in their values and belief systems and their caring of one another throughout all of that. You hope for that in a franchise.

'Part of the reason to come back together is to tell a story but also to come back together because everyone genuinely enjoys working with one another. And it was a really, really positive experience for that reason – other than the fact that I've read the books and loved the books from the very beginning and these characters are extraordinary. It's such an absorbing story that I just felt very lucky, given the unfortunate circumstances surrounding it, that I was just invited in. I hope that *Eclipse* continues this trend of being really reverent of what Stephenie created with the books.'

Although her father, Ron Howard, is one of Hollywood's biggest film directors, she had been kept away from the world of show business. Watching TV was frowned upon and she was instead encouraged to read and play outside. She made her film debut in 2004's *Book of Love*, before starring in a number of films including *The Village*, *Lady in the Water*, *Spider-Man* and *Terminator Salvation*.

She told Radar Online, 'I'm excited to get back to work. I like to work so it's kind of like waiting around getting ready to get back into the game.

'I've been going to the gym and hanging out with friends, and going to rock shows, because when I was up there last time filming *New Moon* I was up there for a while, so in my downtime I try to make sure I stay relaxed.'

Ironically, given Taylor's martial-arts background, we haven't seen much of him as an action star in the series. He was absent from any physical scenes in the first movie, and even in *New Moon* his action scenes were usually computer-generated. While he would do as much of his own stunt work as he could – bar any that might raise insurance issues – the more adrenalin-inducing moments were usually confined to his riding on the dirt bike.

However, that was not through lack of trying. He did say about *New Moon*, 'We did a lot of improv [improvisation] on set. We'd just be in a random forest and, after Jacob transforms, he all of a sudden becomes very agile, and I wanted to show that, because pre-transformation, he's clumsy. But, as soon as he transforms, he's agile. So we'd be in a random forest, and I'd be looking around going, "What can I do to show Jacob's agility in here?"

'Sometimes Chris would be like, "No, Taylor, we don't want you getting hurt, spraining an ankle." But I was like, "Well, how about I just jump off that and then jump through this?" And he was like, "All right, give it a shot."'

Eclipse should change that, however. Just before *New Moon* was released David Slade hinted that he was going to use Taylor's martial-arts prowess on *Eclipse*.

While Lautner may have been annoyed at not doing more stunts, the other members of the Wolf Pack were loving the physical action that *their* characters had to go through. Meraz said, 'The cliff-diving scene was the most fun because the whole Wolf Pack was there and we were jumping off these 50-foot scaffolding things onto an air mattress. It was pretty exciting to be able to do our own stunts.

'[The studio] were pushing for [having stuntmen]; we were pushing against. We wanted to do our own stuff. We had to train for a good two days, eight hours each day just practising jumping, making sure we were landing safely. On the day [of shooting], we were actually jumping from a green-screen cliff, but it was actually taller and a little bit more dangerous because there was foliage and grass on top of it – it was a little slippery. We were fine, and it was really fun.'

(Action is performed in front of a green screen so that post-production computer-generated imagery can be added.)

And making *Eclipse* would be fun for Tyson Houseman, as he finally got to join in the fun. 'The relationship between myself and my cast members really did reflect the relationship of the characters, because when we filmed *New Moon* I was the only character who was not yet part of the Wolf Pack, and so I had a different shooting schedule and different costume work and hair and makeup et cetera.

'While we all became friends, I still did not get to see the rest of the guys as much as they [saw each other], and so they all had a bit more of a bonding experience than I did, although during the filming of *Eclipse* my character is part of the pack, and so I got to spend a lot more time with the guys.'

Keeping the required physical shape needed for Jacob has begun posing difficulties for Lautner. Walking the red carpet at the 2009 Golden Globes, he remarked, 'It's tough. It's a challenge. It's just as hard to keep [the weight] on as it was to put it on originally!'

However, all the effort was worth it and he can't wait for *Twilight* fans to see *Eclipse* in July 2010.

He added that 2009 had been 'really exciting and I'm excited for 2010 – it's going to be a lot of fun. If you've read the books, you know what's coming, it gets good.'

And he's noticed that the attention from the fans hasn't died down. 'It's actually getting bigger and bigger and the fans are still becoming more passionate every day that goes by, which I thought was impossible. But no, we're so used to this now. We've seen everything that these fans can do. So we're not surprised when we see some crazy fan encounter or something. But, yeah, our fans are great, don't get me wrong. It keeps us humble and grounded!'

chapter nine

Wolf Pack's Future Outings

'I don't know where he got it. He's much better at doing it. He's completely handling it.' – Robert Pattinson

The young actor is determined to be Hollywood's next big major star and, with examples of his karate career, his long-haul commutes to try out for auditions and the 'will he/won't he work on *New Moon*?' saga, it's clear that, when Taylor has his heart set on something, you wouldn't bet against his achieving it. He told *Vanity Fair*, 'I'd love to do a movie with Denzel Washington, or some action star such as Matt Damon or Mark Wahlberg would be really cool, too. I love the Bourne series and I wouldn't mind doing something like that.'

And he would get his wish in a new movie called *Abduction* (slated for a 2012 release). The script tells the story of a trained soldier having to save the day when his girlfriend's parents are kidnapped. The spy movie is described as *Bourne Identity* with teenagers.

Lautner is also attached to a film version (again, with a 2012 release) of the rubber-toy *Stretch Armstrong* and a live-action adaptation of the animated TV show *Max Steel* (2010).

Chaske Spencer, meanwhile, is focusing his time on his Urban Dreams production company. 'I want to get scripts for movies I want to do or vehicles to star in or direct. Things are rolling.' He's also adamant that his personal troubles are over but concedes that his number-one fear is that he doesn't want fame to change him. He's determined not to believe 'your own hype'.

With the Wolf Pack around him, they're bound to keep him grounded, however.

Alex Meraz is delighted with the doors that have opened for him following *New Moon*'s success. 'I used to beg for auditions. Now, they're being thrown at me.'

However, he does admit not all of them are in the same class as *New Moon*. 'We're getting a lot of crap!'

He is to show his acting talents, with a part in *Savage Innocent* (2010) – a new movie from the director of cult indie movie *Kids*, Larry Clark.

'Before I got *New Moon*, I'd fight to get auditions. Now I have so many coming my way. I'm happy about that. I actually want to do an action film. I used to be one of those guys that wanted to do wordy actor-y kinds of movies. But now, after seeing *New Moon*, and realising that you can be something bigger than life, transforming into a massive wolf, I'm, like, wow, I want to do an action film, because my background is in martial arts. So anything that involves my holding a gun and killing a crapload of people sounds like a lot of fun.

'I'm sure every film it's going to be like, "OK, this is the scene where your shirt gets ripped off." I'll never be able to keep my shirt on,' he added.

Kiowa Gordon is hard at work on the horror film *Into the Darkness* (2011), while Tyson Houseman and Bronson Pelletier try to pick their next project amid the mountain of scripts that come their way.

The journey has been an intense but crazy, fun one for them, and they hope to seal their relationship by all getting a Wolf Pack tattoo. Said Spencer, 'I don't know if it's going to be an actual Wolf Pack tattoo; we might just design something ourselves. But we're definitely going to get something, because this is a pretty life-changing experience.'

However, there is still the small matter of the last chapter in the *Twilight* saga, *Breaking Dawn*. Asked whether the mammoth story could be condensed into two films, producer Wyck Godfrey told the *LA Times*, 'The issue is not going to be resolved until we get the full treatment and see whether it's organic. If it's not organic, I don't think it will be done, and, if it is, it will be. It really has to do with how much level of detail from the books there is, with all of these new vampires that appear in *Breaking Dawn*, the whole section about Jacob... It's a very long single movie – if it does become a single movie.

'We're just focused on the treatment and getting that right. At that point, we're going to see who's available and who's appropriate. It's such a complicated book because you have the emotions and the intensity of the love story – so you need somebody who's just a wonderful director of actors; and yet it's really complicated from an action and visual-effects standpoint. They've got to have both tools in their kit.'

In fact, there were reports that Meyer was adamant that there would be one movie based on the book and that she had fallen out with the studio over their idea to split it into two films. However, she posted this on her official site:

Just a quick note on the subject of the *Breaking Dawn* film: there is no drama over whether the book should be one movie or two. My personal feeling is that it would be very difficult to cram the whole story into one movie (as I've said in many interviews previous to this), but if a great way of doing that surfaces, I'm all for it. Two or one, whichever way fits the story best is fine by me, and everyone I've spoken with at Summit seems to feel the same way.

We're all excited to move forward on this, and we are slowly and surely getting there. I know people are anxious for news, and so sometimes gossip gets fabricated to stir things up, but there's no basis to this particular story.

One of the more difficult aspects facing the filmmaker is how to bring the character of Bella's half-human/half-vampire daughter Renesmee to life on the big screen. Said Godfrey, 'I keep having visions of *[The Curious Case of] Benjamin Button* in my head [David Fincher's Oscar-winning epic about a man who ages backwards]. It's certainly going to be visual effects in some capacity along with an actor. I wouldn't be surprised if it ends up being a full CG creation, but it also may be a human shot on a soundstage that then is used to shrink down. I don't know. We need a director. When we get a director, that director will need to come with a point of view of how they want to tackle it.'

Taylor Lautner seems to have been born to be Hollywood's next heartthrob and action hero. In fact, there was almost a passing of the baton at 2009's Comic-Con, where, after seeing how Lautner handled the baying fans, Pattinson gushed, 'I don't know where he got it. He's much better at doing it. He's completely handling it. I'm just freaking out all the time. I'm going to end up hitting people and stuff and looking like an idiot.'